Reflecting on the Angeles Arrien.
From A to Z

Compiled by Mickey Eliason in the season of the Warrior,
Winter, 2015/16

Table of Contents

Introduction	3
A is for Awakening	11
B is for Balance	21
C is for Conflict	28
D is for Divine Discontent	41
E is for Equanimity	49
F is for Forgiveness	54
G is for Gratitude	62
H is for Heart	68
I is for "Isn't it interesting?"	75
J is for Judgment	84
K is for Kisses	89
L is for Looping	92
M is for Manifestation	98
N is for Nonattachment	106
O is for Openness	110
P is for Presence	116
Q is for Questing	124
R is for Raven	131
S is for Silence	137
T is for Trust	148
U is for Unbecoming	156
V is for Vision	159
W is for Wisdom	163
X is for Xtra Loving	168
Y is for Yielding	170
Z is for Zen	174
Afterword	177
Resources	180

Introduction

I have such a teacher

Last night my teacher taught me the lesson of poverty, having nothing and wanting nothing.
I am a naked soul standing inside a mine of rubies, clothed in red silk.
I absorb the shining and now I see the ocean, billions of simultaneous motions moving in me.
A circle of lovely, quiet people becomes the ring on my finger,
Then the wind and thunder of rain on the way.
I have such a teacher
--Rumi

Angeles Arrien was the most influential teacher of my lifetime thus far, and I dare say this is true for thousands of others. Like others, I have honored her legacy by continuing the work I started with her. She wanted us to each apply her teachings in ways that best aligned with our own life dreams and gifts and talents. So for myself, I needed to try to integrate the many years of work with her into a new form that could both highlight my progress, and reveal the work I have yet to do. That meant I had to write about the work.

This book is a compilation of my work with Angeles Arrien, primarily in her *Four Fold Way*™ program, but also in dozens of other workshops or personal mentoring sessions. I reviewed my personal journals spanning those 10+ years to pull out the important concepts. This seemed like the best way to integrate the work for myself; to reorganize it into an encyclopedia of the work. Of course, this is the work as filtered through my own understandings of her words at the time, and in reviewing these journals, I could see how much my present circumstances and past understandings of the concepts affected my interpretations. Over time, though, I think I began to grasp the message she intended, even though not all the teachings led to the changes I had hoped for. I cannot guarantee accurate interpretation of Angeles' teaching though, because many of the lessons were open-ended enough to have multiple interpretations and infinite nuance. Ideas that sounded so simple in the moment turned out to be quite complex when I tried to apply them in my life.

I also wrote down ideas that had personal relevance and did not record everything I heard. My own cultural conditioning and background influenced what messages I was able to hear, and what messages seemed too far from my own experience. I was a selective listener. Others who sat in the same circles as I did may have had very different understandings of the same teachings. Others might have recorded content that I could not hear because I had been sent time-traveling by some earlier comment, or that I did not understand or felt was too far from my own cultural background to respectfully incorporate into my own life.

Angeles was a story-teller. Her memory was phenomenal. She had hundreds of teaching stories, insightful catch phrases, famous quotes, and poems in her repertoire. She distinguished between healing stories, those with a lesson learned and full of wisdom; and painful stories of the past that keep us stuck in old ways of thinking and behaving. Her stories were healing.

One of my favorite conversations with fellow students of Angeles Arrien is hearing about how they found the work. These stories are so diverse and interesting, ranging from the rather mundane, such as "A friend recommended it" to the mystical "I had a dream about this work" or "I found a copy of one of Angeles' books on the ground on my way to work and it profoundly changed me." In those conversations with others, I learned that we entered into the work in different life circumstances and transitions, but we were all looking for better ways of being in the world. Many others shared with me that they thought the work was relevant to our lives and potentially useful, even transformative, but took time to engage in it fully because of our own resistances. We all had major insights along the way, and incorporated the teachings into our own lives along our own unique timelines.

My Story

I first encountered the work of Angeles Arrien in 2002, not through Angeles directly, but at a workshop session designed by a man who had attended one of Angeles' programs. He put up posters on the wall of the four archetypes: Warrior, Healer, Visionary, and Teacher, and had us pick our areas of strength. I thought the content was interesting, but didn't care much for the style of the man who was presenting, and pretty quickly forgot about it. A few months later, I was browsing in a bookstore, and found *The Four Fold Way*™. I recognized the title and author and bought the book. It sat in a haphazard pile of unread books on my desk for another six months. Part of the reason that I did no more than leaf through the book was the painful life circumstance I was in. I had been unhappy with some of the aspects of my work for a few years. My life seemed aimless and often joyless. I was in the process of ending a difficult intimate relationship, grieving the loss of my father, and then my sister-in-law died very suddenly at the age of 45. I was not good at asking for help, or revealing my vulnerability by sharing these feelings with others, so I bore this stress mostly alone. I thought I was having a midlife crisis.

Then I went to a conference in Philadelphia in the spring of 2003, and in a casual conversation with a stranger who was seated next to me at dinner, the name Angeles Arrien came up again. This woman, from San Francisco, had been studying with Angeles for several years and held her in the highest regard. Her passion for the work sparked my curiosity and even though we lived 1600 miles apart, I began a friendship with this woman and we continued to converse about the deep work of the *Four Fold Way*™ and how it had transformed the woman's life. She was an important stranger who became a catalyst for my own transformative change. Now when I went home, I read the book. I found it interesting, but did not seem to have a life of its own in the way that this woman had described. I knew I needed to sign up for a workshop and meet this mystery woman, Angeles Arrien. I had learned she was a Basque story-teller. My colleague told me that the book in a written form, although quite powerful in its own right, did not capture the nuances of her stories and

5

teachings. I was told that I had to hear from her in person. The magic was in how she interacted in a group setting.

That summer of 2003, I flew to Arizona for a week-long foundation course, and saw for myself what the work was about: improving one's communication skills, fearlessly addressing the things that hold us back, being more authentic and living one's own life, not the life expected by others. Angeles was unlike anyone I had ever met before. For one thing, the accolades I had heard about her did not prepare me for the petite, pixie-like woman with the quirky sense of humor that I discovered. She used no visual or auditory aids. She merely sat down, usually on the floor, and started to talk, and people were riveted for hours. She did not announce her agenda or offer learning objectives. Instead, she asked questions, and pearls of wisdom dropped from her lips and workshop participants scrambled to capture them on paper. She had a tremendous memory for quotes and poems and research findings. In the many years I worked with her, I never saw her refer to notes or outlines. Angeles held all the knowledge in her head and organized a workshop organically. As she said, "trust in the mystery, but have a back up plan." She used teachable moments to deepen conversations, and led us into small group discussions with questions that took participants out of ego and identities, and into character traits and patterns of responding. She had the ability to cut to the chase and see the central issue that orchestrated a drama or a challenge in a person's life.

I found the work interesting and highly relevant to the crisis of meaning that was happening in my life at the moment. Even though some of the practices were alien to me and a little uncomfortable, I could see the value in them. I came home in an altered state, but living in Iowa, without constant exposure to the work or to a culture or community that supported doing this type of personal growth work, I drifted back into my old ways fairly quickly. Commitments I made to myself during the week in Arizona for changes in my life, though, stuck to the back of my mind and nagged at me from time to time. I started a process of figuring out if I could move from the Midwest to San Francisco. I had never envisioned myself as a city dweller, so I knew I needed a trial run. I scheduled a series of visits, often corresponding with a one-day or weekend workshop in Angeles' Sausalito office, and I dabbled in her work further. I was still on the fringe, knowing the work was important, but not committed to the discipline and rigor I would need to fully engage.

I spent the next year in a major life transition that resulted in moving away from the state where I had lived my entire 50 years thus far, finding a soul mate for the first time in my life and trying to figure out what that meant, and learning to be a west-coaster. Oh yes, and the minor challenges of finding a new job, a new home, and a whole new set of friends. What kept me semi-sane during this time was that I inched my way closer and closer to a full immersion in the personal growth work of Angeles' programs, particularly the *Four Fold Way™*. I also attended workshops on "the second half of life," mentoring, gratitude, writing, and a four weekend program that she co-created with Patrick O'Neill, called *Triumphs of the Imagination,* which in part was about visioning and manifesting break-throughs in one's life. I managed to manifest quite a few---I got temporary work, found an apartment, sold my house in Iowa, and moved for good.

Once I found a permanent job and felt somewhat settled in San Francisco, I joined Angeles' yearlong program in the *Four Fold Way™*, and became a fixture in Angeles' Sausalito teaching room. About two months into the 2014 year-long program, Angeles' health failed and she left her physical body behind on April 24th of 2014. I experienced a grief that was every bit as intense as losing my mother had been the year before. It is hard to explain to people who have not had the privilege of having an extraordinary teacher and mentor just what that loss means. Fortunately, I had a wide circle of other students of Angeles who did understand the impact of that loss, and who supported each other after her death. Angeles' teachings live on through the countless people who encountered her work over her 40 years of teaching and mentoring.

How/Why I Wrote This Book
A few months after Angeles' death, I pulled all of my notebooks from the work with her off of my bookshelves. It was an impressive stack of 14 journals, next to many of Angeles' books: *The Four Fold Way™, Living in Gratitude, The Second Half of Life, The Nine Muses, The Tarot Handbook.* I realized what a treasure trove of wisdom I had acquired over the years. I had been on seven vision quests and had spent more time with Angeles than my own family in the past seven years. Now, how to go about

reflecting on this body of wisdom so I could integrate it? It took another year before the answer came to me.

The inspiration came through another book. I had read a review of David Whyte's *Consolations: The Solace, Nourishment, and Underlying Meaning of Everyday Words.* Before I even finished reading the review, I had downloaded the book to my electronic device. Whyte explored 52 words in beautiful short essays, writing about words like anger, beginning, and solace. So many times while reading this book, I thought of Angeles. Some of the turns of phrase were very similar to the way that Angeles expressed herself. If Angeles were still alive, I would have given her a copy of this book. Then it occurred to me that I could write essays about the words/concepts that were critical to my understanding of the deep work of personal growth; words that came from my years of work with Angeles, transmitted by her oral tradition in stories and seeds of wisdom. I had learned the value of "seeding"—the ability to distill the lessons from an experience without dwelling on the story. Instead of agonizing analysis of a situation from the past, Angeles would probe for the essence of the experience, "But what did you learn from this situation? What are your seeds of learning?" This focus on the seeds leads to tracking what works (and what doesn't work so well) and identifying patterns of behavior that could be changed by seeing where the choice points were. Change was "only a choice away" as Angeles said.

Every year after a vision quest (a 2 day, 3 night experience in solitude and silence in nature), Angeles would suggest that we do a creative work: a collage, a painting, a poem, a story, or some other form of artistic creation that helped us to integrate our experience. For me, it was almost always a story. Angeles opened me up to creative writing and restored the sense of humor that I had all but lost in my midlife crisis. I include some of those vision quest integration stories in this book.

But Angeles died before that final years' vision quest, and I was left feeling unfinished and incomplete. The idea that Angeles might be a mortal being who could die was an inconceivable notion to me. This book represents the healing power of reflection and integration of the year or so since of dealing with the grief of Angeles' passing. It also sums up all the joyous years before that, as I learned more about aligning my self with my values, about being in relationship with others, and about trusting in the mystery but always having a backup plan.

For each letter, from A to Z, I select one word to write about in some depth, and then briefly define other words that stemmed from the teaching. The essays include both Angeles' teaching and sometimes reference to other authors or my own reflection on how the concept played out in my own life. The definitions in the glossary, though, mostly come directly from my notes on Angeles' teaching. I invite you to write about the words that trigger, surprise, challenge, or inspire you! As you read, keep in mind Angeles' question, "What's working ya?"

Some of the deepest work happened in group sessions as we grappled with the lessons in collective, so I draw from my notes over the years to pull out examples, stories, and discussion questions that Angeles posed to help us "deepen, soften, strengthen, and open" about each quality. *The Four Fold Way*™ book contains the foundation of this work, so this book is not a replacement, but rather, a supplement to it. Each year Angeles added to the teachings so I focus on the content of my notes from group sessions here. If content appeared more than once, I have not noted a year, but for activities or content that was unique to only one program or session, I have noted when it was introduced.

Acknowledgements

I dedicate these essays and glossary to Angeles, whom I hope would say, "Good tracking!" I acknowledge that this book is Angeles' intellectual creation; all I did was organize the teaching in a different way (an innovation; not a creative project). I also acknowledge that every person who sat in a circle with me in one of Angeles' on-going groups or one-time workshops contributed to my understanding of the work. I equally value the ones who frustrated me because they didn't seem to "get it" or who told long stories that had me fidgeting with boredom. From them, I learned about my own judgments and deepened my practice of patience. I learned from those who were already wise with life experience and who could share it in a way that I could hear and apply to my own life. I learned from others who were able to be vulnerable in the group in a way that frightened me, and I was thankful for how their example helped me to open up more. I learned much from the ones whose motives I questioned when they spoke, because they often turned out to be mirrors of my own ulterior motives. I appreciated the sense of humor that always bubbled up in the midst of the challenging hard work we were doing. And many of the "important strangers" modeled grounding, integrity, respect, and effective ways of communicating that put the teaching into practice. I would like to extend deep gratitude to Patrick O'Neill who was a co-teacher with Angeles in some of the programs I attended and who has generously and magnificently continued the work after Angeles' death. He has modeled the path of turning grief into service to others. Finally, I belong to a very deep group of people who were working with Angeles in her last few years, and who continue to meet twice a month to deepen our learning: Louis, Meigs, Karen, Pat, Marcia, and Gaye. Thanks for keeping me deep in the work and modeling commitment to a rigorous daily practice.

What Is Your Story?
What is your experience with the work with Angeles Arrien? How did you find this work? How did it transform you? How are you continuing to honor her legacy of teachings?

A is for Awakening

The first step to personal growth is getting out of the rut of living a mundane, automatic life, and learning to pay attention to the present moment, the moment when life is lived. Some call it mindfulness; others call it paying attention or waking up. The dictionary defines awakening as:

> *An adjective*
> 1. rousing; quickening:
>
> *A noun*
> 2. the act of awaking from sleep.
> 3. a revival of interest or attention.
> 4. a recognition, realization, or coming into awareness of something: a rude awakening to the disagreeable facts.
> 5. a renewal of interest in religion, especially in a community; a revival.

Being awake, in Angeles' program was some combination of the dictionary definitions—a rousing, a restoring of one's awareness and awe of the world around us (revival of interest/attention), a coming into awareness of the state of our own hearts and soul (recognition of something), and an exploration of the mysterious forces of nature and spirit (a revival). Many of us are not really fully awake to our own lives and are just going through the motions, or living our lives to meet the expectations of others. Angeles referred to the state of marching through life without awareness as the "procession of the living dead."

I had been in that company for a few years before my move; a work-aholic very successfully doing the things I was expected to do, but not really present to my own life. I had glimmers of a life lived in the present when I worked in my garden. With my hands in the earth, I felt connected to something bigger than myself. But in my intimate relationship, I was numb from the effort of trying to figure out how to extricate myself from a big mistake I had made a few years earlier. I distracted myself from my unhappiness with constant, but often meaningless, activity. I had to re-awaken to save my own spirit.

One of Angeles' favorite poems about awakening came from Rumi:

> The breezes at dawn have secrets to tell you
> > Don't go back to sleep!
> You must ask for what you really want.
> > Don't go back to sleep!
> People are going back and forth across the doorsill where the
> two worlds touch, The door is round and open
> > Don't go back to sleep!

The door, round and open, exists in many forms. For some, it is through a religious practice. That route had not worked for me for many years. Others enter the door through meditation or spending time in nature. Angeles recommended an hour in nature every day to help stay connected to the earth, and awaken to its beauty. That was the portal that most spoke to me, and moving to California allowed me to spend so much more time outdoors in awe of the natural beauty of the area: the sweeping ocean views, the golden foothills and granite mountains, the lush, Mediterranean landscapes of San Francisco, the golden and red grape vines in fall. Even the man-made wonders, such as the many bridges, were portals to awe and wonder. Beauty is one of the alarm clocks that can awaken the sleeper. David Whyte put it this way: *"Beauty is the harvest of presence."* That is, beauty can be both the catalyst to awakening, and awakening can open us up to see the beauty that is around us every day. If we are present and aware, it's there.

Awakening can also be of the "rude" type. Many of us, once we are fully present to our own lives, recognize the unhealthy patterns that need our attention. I certainly experience those challenging awakening moments on a regular basis now when I revert back to some old pattern in a time of conflict or fatigue. Rumi's advice, "don't go back to sleep" is a reminder to us all to stay awake in the face of all the life circumstances that try to put us back to sleep: the tedium of daily repetitive activities like laundry and long commutes in traffic, the sensory overload of media that assaults us 24/7 from our electronic devices, and the fatigue of daily living. Most of all, the internal chatter in our own heads is a threat to being awake and present to the lived moment. That internal conversation takes us from the distant past to the remote future in a matter of seconds—a word, an image, a person in front of us, a scent, a song, can trigger this time-traveling and put the rest of our bodies into automatic pilot. Angeles recommended rigorous daily practices to constantly bring our attention back to the present, the moment where life is lived. For me, the practice of spending one hour in nature per day reminds me to stay awake and live my life in the present moment. Thank you, Angeles, for making me aware of how important it is to spend quality time by myself in nature every day. This practice changed my life.

What's your experience with awakening? How do you stay awake? What triggers you to go back to sleep?

"A" Glossary

The 5 A's. Angeles often facilitated a small group activity where she had participants reflect on the 5 A's from David Richo's *How to be An Adult in Relationship:*

1. *Attention.* When we stay attuned to the present moment and observe, listen, and notice the feelings that arise, we are awake in our relationship.
2. *Acceptance.* To be an adult means to acknowledge that my partner and I are good, just as we are. This means not trying to change our significant others.
3. *Appreciation.* When we give thanks for all our gifts, our limits, our longings, and our human condition, we strengthen our relationships.
4. *Affection.* How do I show my partner how I feel through words, holding, and touching in respectful ways? Do I show my love through my actions?
5. *Allowing.* This is the recognition that life and love are good just as they are, with all their joys and pains. Give up trying to take control. This is related to Angeles' concept of nonattachment.

Angeles would ask us to consider which of the A's were present in our current relationships, and which ones needed some work, or were challenging for us. How would our relationships be different if we fully engaged in all five of the A's?

Abundance. Angeles said that our natural state is one of abundance rather than scarcity. We have unlimited love, compassion, flexibility, and other resources for our needs, and to share with others. Scarcity puts us into comparison, competition, clinging, or withholding.

Acknowledgment. This is one of the arms of love. To love someone, you must acknowledge what that person means to you and what they have done to enhance your life. Who needs acknowledging in your life? This keeps significant others in our lives from feeling taken for granted.

Action. "Action absorbs anxiety," Angeles always said. She added that hope promotes action and apathy promotes stasis. Insights require actions, otherwise they are like floating clouds and dissipate. Breakthroughs are only possible through some witness-able actions. In my 2012 journal, I found reference to the Pygmy tribes of the rainforest, who had a saying, "Be brave, start small, do something you enjoy, and don't overcommit." Angeles' programs were not just based on abstract ideas; rather she constantly taught and urged us to practice daily actions to change old patterns and create a better future.

Addictions. These are the shadow side of the healer (shadows are unacknowledged or unwanted characteristics that we have, but hide or bury), and can include:

- Addiction to perfectionism: not being able to complete a task because it's never good enough. Perfectionism in relationships dehumanizes the other person, and leads to loss of humanity. The other side of perfectionism is excellence, beauty, and the ability to learn from one's mistakes, as well as leadership.
- Addiction to a need to know. This involves not being able to make a decision until you feel you have enough information—and there's never enough information. This is a control dynamic and fosters expertise (staying in your comfort zone) rather than mastery (always wanting to go to a higher level). The other side of the need to know is wisdom (clarity and discernment).
- Addiction to the drama/intensity. This involves a tendency to stir things up unnecessarily to feel alive or needed. This person exaggerates, indulges, controls, and overanalyzes. They may falsely label peace as boring, or a sign that another person does not care. They enlist a lot of other people in the drama to get attention, and often take the victim stance (the martyr). Some are quite skilled at this and appear charming on the surface because they use seduction and more subtle strategies to control others. Others appear as needy and helpless, and often attract those who swoop in to save the day (the rescuers). The other side of addiction to intensity is the passionate heart that does not go into drama or collapse and is capable of love and generosity.
- Addiction to what's not working. This is attachment and over-identification with the problem and becomes self-fulfilling. The other side is vision and intuition—being

15

able to see the whole as well as the parts. Usually much more in our lives is working than not working. We can transfer skills from the places that are working.

Alignment. Angeles discussed alignment in many contexts. It could be the alignment of head, heart, and gut when making important decisions, or the alignment of one's work with values and life purpose, or alignment of words with intentions and behaviors. Life is a continual process of alignment. Where am I out of balance? Where am I attached to outcomes? What am I trying to control? Do I over-rely on my mind and ignore "gut feelings"?

Allurement. Angeles described the things we draw to us as our "field of allurement." These are our life dreams and they carry creative fire. The natural state is abundance; the unnatural state of scarcity fosters greed and hoarding. When in abundance, we draw the resources we need and the positive energy from others and the environment.

Ancestors. Angeles talked of the role of ancestors in supporting us and often said, "The ancestors love an assignment." She invoked them before doing journey work or meditations, and asked us to put a male ancestor behind us on the right, a female ancestor behind us on the left, and helper allies at our feet as we posed an issue we wanted to work on. She taught us that in many cultures, healers would say that the ancestors proposed, "Maybe this is the one who will change the unhealthy family patterns," and encourage us to be the one. The ancestors support us in making these changes. In my 2008 notes, I wrote that Angeles said if you wake up between midnight and 2 am, it is because an ancestor visited.

Anger. Anger is an acknowledgment of a violation of limits and boundaries. It is not harmful unless aimed at someone with blame. Anger is a response to an injustice, betrayal, or disappointment. If we get angry about little things, it is often because these have been the source of repeated disappointment. We can only get angry about something we care about. Anger stems from fear: and what we fear will manifest again if we don't address it. When we are angry, we are in a reactive state, and should not take action or make decisions. If we are with others when we get angry, we can tell them that we are not reliable at the moment and need time to process. Eleanor Roosevelt said "Anger is one letter from danger." Sometimes we use anger as a way of handling fear or hurt feelings. To stay in anger for a prolonged time, though, is a form of indulgence. We need to feel it, acknowledge it, and then take action to dispel it, before it moves into danger.

Animal Spirits. Angeles noted that animals that we love, who appear regularly to us, or show up in journey work, are here to support our work. Water animals symbolize heart work and emotional transitions; scaled creatures symbolize intuition, instincts and wisdom. Winged creatures are the bridge between the inner and outer worlds.

Appeasement. The dictionary defines the word "appease" as:
    1. to bring to a state of peace or quiet : calm
    2. to cause to subside : allay <*appeased* my hunger>
    3. to pacify, conciliate; *especially* : to buy off (an aggressor) by concessions usually at the sacrifice of principles.

Angeles focused on the third definition, the one that is damaging to our personhood. Appeasing is a behavior of the conflict avoider who wants to keep the peace—thus attracting controllers. Appeasing results in giving up pieces of the self to others, giving away power, and reducing self-respect. It contributes to the false-self because we are hiding our true feelings from the person we appease. That person also loses respect for us when they discover we have been appeasing rather than being honest with them. It leads to a sacrifice of our principles, so we also lose self-respect.

Apology. Angeles often talked about genuine apology as offering both an expression of being sorry for causing harm to another, but paired with a promise that the behavior would not happen again. Regretting hurting someone without the commitment to change is not a genuine apology. Excessive apology comes from guilt. We can tell when an apology is genuine, because it comes from the heart and is clear and concise.

Approval Needs. Far too many of us do things to get approval from others, not because we really want to behave this way. It is a way of giving away power and pieces of the authentic self. It stems from one of the basic assumptions that we have to release: that our happiness is dependent on others.

Archetype. Angeles' *Four Fold Way™* program is based on the idea that every indigenous culture has at least these four archetypes, or sets of characteristics that make up a person. In Jung's philosophy, an archetype is an inherited way of thinking and being. Everyone has elements of all four archetypes, but they tend not to be balanced. A balanced person can draw on all of these resources to lead a more authentic life that is aligned with one's life dreams and uses all their gifts and talents. The *Four Fold Way™* is a program that aimed to strengthen our resources and sufficiency in all four archetypes. The four archetypes are summarized below.

Archetype	Characteristics	Principle
Warrior	Leadership skills, right use of power, knowing what we stand for and by. Sets limits and boundaries, respects self and others. The warrior is associated with the north, and with winter.	Show up and be present
Healer	Uses the healing power of love, care for inner self and outer world. The healer is associated with the south and the spring.	Pay attention to what has heart and meaning
Visionary	Sees the big picture, lives in one's truth and authenticity. Vision brings our creative fire into the world. The visionary is associated with the east, and with summer.	Tell the truth without blame or judgment
Teacher	Wisdom stems from trust and is flexible and fluid. Objectivity and nonattachment are compassionate ways of caring deeply. The teacher is associated with the west and the fall.	Be open, not attached to outcomes

After my first vision quest in 2008, this story about the challenges of developing all the archetypes came to me.

Archetype Mania

Is anyone else having trouble integrating their archetypes? Does anyone else feel like they have multiple archetype personality disorder? Let me give you an example of what I mean. Yesterday my warrior was engaged in standing meditation in the corner when the visionary rushed in all excited, yelling, "It's at the gate-- we have to find the truth without blame or judgment right now. I need you to be fully present and help me."

Startled by the strident tone of the visionary's comments, and by the violation of the warrior's limits and boundaries, the healer jumped in between them. "No, no," she cried, "the truth can be heartless at the wrong time or place. Stop and reflect about what has heart and meaning. Stay in noble silence if your heart is not clear." The warrior sneered, "This is no time for namby-pamby nurturing and reflecting, we need to take an action to absorb the visionary's anxiety—look at her, she's losing her funny bone."

The visionary started to sing her power song so the warrior took out her rattle in an attempt to drown her out. The noise was beginning to annoy the neighbors, the important strangers next door and the "Yeah-buts" upstairs. The ancestor spirits and helper allies were shaking their heads in dismay and muttering, "please, just say what is so when it's so." The healer, appalled by the conflict and the visionary's off-key singing, dropped to the floor into a cradling position, clutching her chest and whimpering, "Oh, my weak heart." The visionary said in an exasperated tone, "You have always been addicted to intensity."

Suddenly the warrior looked around, "Hey, where's that teacher. She always detaches when we need some wisdom around here." At that moment, the teacher entered the room, calmly and quietly surveyed the chaos and announced, "Well that's a story that didn't need to happen. We have some shadow work to do." They all embraced, vowed to work together, and threw kisses at each other, because you can't be grumpy, mad, or sad when you throw kisses.

Arrogance. The shadow side of self-sufficiency can be unhealthy pride and arrogance. Arrogance is a position of superiority to others that comes from comparison and competition. It can also be associated with a need to be right.

Attachment. Where we become too attached to a certain outcome, we lose our flexibility and move into a fixed perspective. This closes off creativity, alternative possibilities, and makes us rigid and humorless. Where you have lost your sense of humor and are too serious, is where your attachment work lies. We all have three kinds of attachments to release on a daily basis:
1. the need to control
2. the attachment to possessions or how I look
3. the need for self-importance

Authenticity. One of the major goals of this personal/spiritual work is to let our authentic self emerge, shedding all the masks and false-self systems that we have developed over time to get the approval of others, or to survive in hostile, frightening climates. We take on roles and identities much like actors in a play. When we retrieve the lost parts of ourselves, and speak from our own inner wisdom voice, we can be our authentic selves. In 2009, I wrote down this quote from Angeles: "Who we think we are is a belief to be undone." Our authenticity gets tested in two ways; 1) how we handle conflict, and 2) whether we engage in appeasing and pleasing others. In 2013, Angeles said, "Only when you can meet the self that is feared, can you meet the self that is."

What "A" words speak to you? What is your work at this time?

B is for Balance

For most of my adult life, I had heard about balance and achieving just the right blend of work and play; drudgery and pleasure; obligations and fun. I had been told in so many ways that the successful life was balanced. Yet my work setting sent out a different message--I was to be 100% committed to my job and produce, produce, produce, or lose the job. I was in the 'publish or perish' world of academics. The emphasis on productivity and concrete deliverables meant that I learned to ignore and devalue being, and focused on the doing. I learned to over-value the products of the mind, and shut down my intuition and feelings. I yearned for more balance in my life when I moved to California, and I did spend more time in nature, in silent reflection, and in just being by myself or with others. However, I had not really embraced the concept of balance. I thought of balance as a state that I could achieve and stay within indefinitely. That is, once I reached this mythical state of balance, my work would be done.

One day before a session with Angeles, I was watching surfers on Rodeo Beach, and it occurred to me that balance is a continual process of adjusting one's course. Like the surfer, no one is ever truly in balance for more than a split second. Now balance sounded like a lot of work of constantly monitoring one's situation and making adjustments. Then I read David Whyte's ideas on "work/life balance," which he called a "phrase that often becomes a lash with which we punish ourselves." He goes on to critique the whole idea of balance:

> "The current understanding of work-life balance is too simplistic. People find it hard to balance work with family, family with self, because it might not be a question of balance. Some other dynamic is in play, something to do with a very human attempt at happiness that does not quantify different parts of life and then set them against one another. We are collectively exhausted because of our inability to hold competing parts of ourselves together in a more integrated way." (From *The Three Marriages: Reimagining work, self and relationship*).

This made a lot of sense; work is part of life, part of life is work. If the two were integrated, so that the time spent in work was doing meaningful activity, one's life was good. Rather than obsess over the hours (am I adequately balancing time at work with time spent in life?) the question was more one of how was I spending my time in general. Did that time feed my soul? The balance was between doing the things that were necessary for my survival, but did not feed the soul, and highly meaningful activities aligned with my life purpose and goals. So I had to balance washing dishes with deep conversations, and paying the bills with creative writing, and recording grades with mentoring students. I found ways to make the tedious jobs more meaningful by meditating through washing dishes and folding clothes. I got into the habit of putting a current problem or issue for which I needed guidance in my mind before starting a beach walk. Most of the time, by the time the walk was over, I had solved the problem. I reduced the amount of time that the television was turned on, so did not add to my burden/stress with materialistic cravings or superficial messages. Now, more of the hours of my day were meaningful.

I came back to the image of the surfer and re-imagined the task. A surfer becomes one with the sea (aligning inner and outer worlds) and must have sharpened awareness of the nature of waves (be fully present). Deep connection with the sea and integration of body, mind, and spirit must occur to stay on one's board, with constant negotiation of changing conditions (tracking/vigilance) and full engagement with the experience from beginning to end. When one episode of life is over, be ready for the next one—waves crest and spill over, and then the process repeats, but not in exactly the same way. Each wave has its own character and we must adapt to the changes. The joy of the surfer was in the particulars with each unique wave—keeping balance was not "work," but part of the fun.

During my reflections on this essay, I realized how much of my journals in the past few years had focused on balance, but I could not actually remember Angeles discussing the concept of balance using that word. She talked more about alignment. But she did emphasize having at least an hour a day in silence and solitude in nature, slowing down to nature's rhythm, and she encouraged a daily ritual of practices to center and ground one's self. If I did all of those, my life would be balanced. That is, alignment might be one of the qualities that must be considered in balancing one's life.

One day, I tried to put *Four Fold Way*™ concepts to the image of surfing, and called it "aquanimity." The north, right use of power, was related to tapping into the power of the ocean and the wave to work with it, not against it. The south, the healing force, is associated with fluidity and flexibility, the main characteristics of water. The east, the visionary, involves the ability to see the big picture of the characteristics of the wave and my location on the board and changing winds and tides. Finally, the west, the wisdom way, helps me to not attach to outcome. I go with the flow on this ride. This image, made as one of my vision quest integration art projects, is on the wall in my office, reminding me to monitor and realign my sense of balance through-out the day.

Aquanimity: Surfing Life's Challenges

What is your relationship to the concept of balance?

"B" Glossary

Beauty. The beauty of nature, and using nature images to reflect on our experiences comes out in many forms in Angeles' teaching, from writing haiku to seeding experiences on vision quests. Angeles urges us to find "the good, the true, and the beautiful" in ourselves and in others. Beauty brings us into the present moment. Some objects, like certain flowers, are a fleeting beauty that last only a few days, showing the impermanence of things and the value of appreciating them in the moment. The vibrant green of spring is a healing energy. Beauty of any type is a healing agent. Angeles asked us to consider these questions: Where has beauty captured my attention this year? What types of beauty am I drawn to? Beauty is a catalyst that opens the heart and nurtures the spirit. The beauty way is a daily practice of following what has heart and meaning.

Befriending. Angeles used this term often, in the context of self-love and personal growth. To grow and develop our personhood, we have to befriend the shadow side as well as our gifts and talents. This may involve a need for self-forgiveness. Three habits that get in the way of befriending are 1) judging myself (critical self-talk); 2) assuming others are judging me; and 3) comparing myself to others.

Questions that Angeles asked to facilitate befriending work include:

- Under what circumstances do I judge myself? What are the triggers?
- What do I think others judge me about?
- Who or what in the past year triggered comparison or competition? On the other side of comparison is my own self worth.
- Where do I have doubts?
- How quickly do I re-balance after challenging events?
- Every conversation ignites a different part of myself, or brings out a different aspect of my personhood, gifts and talents, or shadow. Who/what draws out my [fill in the blank: compassion, anger, humor, intelligence, playfulness, judgment, impatience, etc.].

Bell Work. Angeles pointed out that the clear tone of a bell is a sign to wake up. Bell work can be done to bring us to the present moment. Angeles said that in many indigenous cultures, the bell is known as "the sound that demons cannot stand." It is the sound of clarity. The bell is the tool of the visionary.

Be Yourself. Angeles loved to quote Oscar Wilde: "Be yourself; everyone else is taken." This idea is related to authenticity and identifying the need for soul retrieval. We have to retrieve lost parts of ourselves to return to our authentic nature. In terms of intimate relationships, she said it was best to be yourself, because it would only hurt once if rejected. If we first enter a relationship presenting a false self, we can get rejected twice; once for the false mask, then again for the real self who was not courageous enough to present itself in the first place!

Body Wisdom. Angeles said that there are three outer points to access body wisdom. The forehead symbolizes the place of the mind, consciousness, the senses, and information. The chest holds the heart, the center of emotions and the life breath. It needs to be open to hold wisdom. The belly is the home of the gut, the center of trust, intuition, and instinctual knowledge. These three body parts are connected by the skeleton, which symbolizes the bones of the earth. If all three are aligned and congruent, we can challenge the self-critic and access the wisdom voice. A clear mind sets limits on the doubting voices, and an open heart helps us to show up strong and clear. Our voice/throat reveals if the mind and heart are connected. If we speak in a clear voice with resonance and fire, we are aligned. The belly is the home of trust, and accessing intuition. Standing meditation strengthens self-trust.

Bones. Angeles pointed out that we should stay attached to our bones (be grounded) to stay authentic:
- our backbone: the power and strength within us
- our wish bone: the goals/dreams that we have
- our funny bone: our sense of humor
- the hollow little bone that symbolizes the mystery

Boundaries. In Angeles' teaching, this concept was always linked with another: limits and boundaries. To stand in our own authenticity and power, we need to be distinguished from others, have limits that cannot be compromised, and boundaries that show what we stand for. When we are clear with others about our limits and boundaries, we create safety. Honoring other people's limits and boundaries is a sign of respect.

Braiding. Angeles often talked of a prophesy of indigenous peoples: *"When the wisdom of the sky and the wisdom of the earth are braided through the human heart, then there will be a rainbow of people."* Braiding the old and the new leads to something entirely new that embraces the old rather than just replaces it. Angeles often expressed hope that we were close to fulfilling this prophesy through all the communications technologies that connect people and ideas, as well as the new movements to save the earth and conserve the natural wonders—as people from around the world come together, we are creating that rainbow of diverse peoples working together.

Break My Heart. Another favorite saying from Rumi that Angeles often repeated was "Oh, break my heart, oh break my heart again, that I might love even more." In other words, loss opens us to even greater capacity for love in the future.

Breakthrough: In each new year, Angeles urges us to set sacred intentions for a breakthrough; a witness-able change in behavior. We get breakthroughs when we are able to listen to our heart and not be deceived by the cleverness of our minds. Angeles always said, "Progress is not a breakthrough." Breakdowns are learning opportunities that can mobilize breakthroughs. At the beginning of every new year, Angeles asked "What is the breakthrough you would like to create and manifest this year?"

A breakthrough is more than just having a change in perspective, and requires a manifestation of some sort, as she noted in an interview:

> *"The Navajo has a wonderful term for a great realization or insight that is not sustained: they call it a floating cloud...It's beautiful in its shape and we describe it and talk about it—and then it dissipates because it hasn't been mobilized or grounded or sustained...We're generating a lot of floating clouds. We need to ground our ideas so they can change the world...Nothing changes unless it's grounded and it's manifested." Angeles Arrien (in Schlitz, Vieten, & Amorok, 2007, Living Deeply: The art and science of transformation in everyday life)*

26

Bridging. Angeles was a bridger: a connector of cultures and diverse ideas and people. She said that bridges were a symbol of creativity, and living in the Bay Area with so many bridges was to live in a land that sparked creativity of all sorts. A bridge is a two way process, so the bridger is enriched as much as the people or ideas that she bridges.

Building A Case. Sometimes, when we have had a conflict or feel annoyed by something a family member, significant other, or coworker has said or done, we go into a mode of making it bigger than it needs to be. Like the prosecuting attorney, we build our case about the wrong-doing of the perpetrator, and our resentment builds up. This signals a case of attachment to a certain outcome and forecloses the possibility of entertaining alternatives. Sometimes we do this when we fail to check in with the other person about what their behavior or words meant. This idea of building a case also shows the danger of repeating the old painful stories—with each telling, we continue to build the case against the perpetrator and lose the details about our own part in the initial conflict. The story takes on a life of its own and continues to hurt us and affect our current behavior and state of mind. Whenever I'm building a case, I'm avoiding my own path of change.

What "B" words speak to you? What is your work at this time?

C is for Conflict

A big lesson for me over the decade of working with Angeles has been acknowledging the degree to which conflict avoidance has affected my life and well-being. Before I moved to California, I was in a painful five-year relationship that could have ended in the first year had I not been so conflict avoidant. I always thought of conflict as a bad thing; something to be avoided at all costs. Conflict meant the loss of relationships, a win or lose situation, a distressing condition that made me so uncomfortable that I had a fight or flight reaction. In my case, it was always flight. Conflict was an argument, a clash, or a disagreement. None of these things sounded positive to me, but rather, events to be carefully avoided. My stoic Midwestern upbringing had emphasized a "don't rock the boat" style of interactions with others. So I developed skills of appeasement and demonstrated a passive/aggressive style for most of my life.

Angeles said that our families are the training ground for learning conflict and communication. I think both of my parents, and many of the other adults in my life modeled conflict avoidance, and I "normalized the abnormal" by thinking that conflict avoidance was the only way to behave in uncomfortable situations.

I had never heard the definition of conflict that Angeles offered: **an opportunity for creative problem-solving.** I still have trouble thinking of conflict as a positive event, but I certainly recognize how much my conflict avoidance has damaged my life, from lack of self-respect when I gave in to keep the peace or when I disappointed people I cared about by not standing up for myself or others. Conflict avoidance kept me from being my authentic self, and took me out of my own integrity. So how does one face conflict directly and courageously? I have the "deer in the headlights" syndrome when faced with a conflict, at least when the other person is someone who I love, respect or who has authority over me. I freeze, I get a lump the size of a walnut in my throat that prevents even a squeak to emerge, and my heart pounds. My thoughts become a jumble of confusion. In that physical and mental state, it is hard to focus on the situation at hand. I'm taken out of the present moment and my primitive reptilian brain takes over and urges me to "get the hell out of here."

At the 2013 vision quest, I did have an insight about the "deer in the headlights" phenomenon. I was watching actual deer grazing on the hillside below me, picking their way through the golden grasses. They would freeze when startled by a noise or movement around them. I realized that it is a natural state to stop and assess whether there is danger. But if there is no real physical danger, it's important to move on. Where I have problems is getting caught up in my own thoughts and manufactured fears that keep me frozen for too long.

On top of the conflict avoidance, I am a slow processer whenever a situation is emotionally charged. I feel discomfort and distress, but it takes time to sort out the actual underlying feeling and the appropriate response. Angeles recommended just sitting with the discomfort, waiting for the answer to arise about what the feeling state might be. She promoted deep listening to understand the other person's perspective. I studied non-reactive responses to conflict, approaching it with curiosity rather than fear. I still find it very challenging to just feel the discomfort and wait it out, when there is an angry or demanding person in my face.

Angeles recommended a guideline for dealing with conflict in a timely fashion: the 24/3/7 rule. That is, ideally, a conflict should be addressed within 24 hours. If you are a slow processer, it might take 3 days to sort it out. If you don't address it within seven days, the problem becomes yours, not the person with whom you have the conflict. You have to let it go. I am learning how hard it is to re-engage with the conflict after a day or more has passed—it takes a lot of courage to contact a person and say that I want to discuss what happened and resolve the issue. It's still the easier road in the short term to avoid the conflict, but it is to the detriment of the relationship to do so. I am working on my own self-trust to know that I can handle the conflict at the time it happens, or within three days at the most.

Once Angeles said that if we "say what is so when it's so," we can reduce conflict by 50%. Doing what I say I will do can reduce another chunk of conflict. I think I am moving toward better communication so that conflict can be reduced. But I still have work to do in the moment of a conflict when it is face-to-face. Every time it has happened in the past few years, it seems that all the lessons learned from Angeles disappear just when I need them most, and I slip into an old mode. I don't recognize that I have shifted back to my old pattern until it's over. My fear of conflict is so deeply ingrained that I automatically move into old ways of being so quickly that I miss the choice point.

I found a curious statement in the 2008 journal: "Conflict avoidant people are not able to see themselves clearly." Maybe that is why it is hard for me to see my own patterns and reactions when I am in the reactive moment of conflict. Outside of that moment, though, I am strengthening. As I focus more on what's working, I think I am slowly transferring those skills to conflict situations. I think I am seeing myself more clearly now most of the time, but without the guidance of a teacher or an objective outside observer, I'm not sure if I'm deluding myself.

Another big insight I had recently was the idea that I may avoid conflict so that I do not appear to be a critical or judgmental person to others. Conflict avoidance is a way of hiding my shadow side. Because I am so conflict averse, and react strongly to people who are "in-your-face" conflict engagers, perhaps they are mirroring my own judgmental nature back to me?

At a 2003 workshop on conflict resolution, Angeles offered a process for negotiating difficult situations called the Four Point International Negotiation Tool. Before meeting face-to-face with the others involved in the conflict, clarify these issues for yourself first:

1. How do I see this issue between us and what is my perspective on what needs to be done?
2. How do I feel about this issue? State to the other "I feel that..." and follow with a statement of fact, not judgment or evaluation.
3. What do I want?
4. What am I willing to do to resolve this? What am I not willing to do (what are my limits and boundaries around this issue)?

When the parties come together to discuss the conflict, each shares their views on the four points, without countering or arguing. One should never ask "why" during negotiations, because this is a perspective of defensiveness and sounds accusatory. If the feelings match (step 2), then a negotiation is possible. Then go on to what each party wants—if there is willingness, you may be able to resolve the issue. When the differences are irreconcilable, then apology and reparation work is needed. If the conflict is resolved, trust will need to be rebuilt.

Angeles, thank you for the questions that brought me this far on the journey to overcome my conflict avoidance. I wish you were here to challenge me further as I try to find my way.

How do you deal with conflict? Are you an avoider or able to face conflict with little fear?

"C" Glossary

Center. Angeles often referred to our center or core as the seat of all learning; where we integrate and deepen our character. It is the inner version of the formidable middle. It is symbolized in various cultures by the center of a circle, a medicine wheel, a gate or threshold, the lodge pole, or as a cross (the cross-cultural integration symbol). In my 2013 journal, Angeles recommended that we choose a centering prayer. Pick a word that feels sacred; peace, love, trust, harmony, etc., and chant or sing it when feeling fear, anxiety, or out of balance. We can also use a focus on our breath or heartbeat to bring us back to our center. In our group sessions, Angeles always had a basket of flowers in the center of the circle to remind us of the healing power of beauty. Beauty can bring us back to our center as well.

Clarity. Being clear and simple in one's communications is clarity; being clear about a decision without waffling or doubt. These are core qualities to building trust and creating safety for ourselves and for others. If we are not clear about some issue, we should not make decisions or take actions. We need time in silence and at nature's rhythm to access the wisdom voice. A clear "I don't know" is also possible.

Change. Angeles believed in the ability of every person to change. If they did not change, it was because they did not want to change. She tried to help people see what they were getting out of not changing (pleasing or appeasing others, to get sympathy, holding on to a victim status, feeling special) or what was holding them back from changing (fear usually, sometimes expectations of partners or family). People change for two reasons; 1) they cannot stand it anymore; or 2) they are deeply moved or seized by a fire/passion. Sometimes we are too close to it to recognize the changes we are making. One poem that Angeles was fond of sharing about the nature of change was this.

> *My boat struck something deep; nothing happened*
> *Waves, water, silence*
> *Nothing happened ?*
> *Perhaps everything has happened and I'm standing*
> *in the middle of my new life.*
> *--Juan Ramon Jimenez*

Checking In. Often we make assumptions about what another person's words or behaviors mean and rush to judgment. Angeles pointed out that often we erroneously believe that their actions/words had something to do with us, when they did not, or that we have misinterpreted them. Whenever we say to ourselves, "I wonder what he meant by that" or feel uneasy about the words or behaviors, it is best to go to the person as soon as possible to check it out. Preferably, we check it out within 24 hours or 3 days, but no later than 7 days.

Chi of Writing. In my 2013 journal, there is a note about the 8 energies of chi that govern writing. There were movements that went with each phase. The 8 energies are:
- Gather (pulling together materials needed for writing)
- Rise (rise into an outline)
- Expand (come up with examples and write them down)
- Contract (edit, sharpen)
- Flow in (write for yourself, not others)
- Flow out (let others read it)
- Settle (develop the final draft)
- Disperse (publish, disseminate your writing)

Choice Points. Every day, we make hundreds of choices. Some of these come after deliberate, conscious decision-making, but many of them are automatic or habitual responses, related to old patterns. If we can be present to each moment, we can recognize when we are making a choice stemming from old unhealthy patterns. We can break those patterns by making a different decision—"it's only a choice away."

Circle. The circle is a universal symbol of unity and wholeness. When we sit in a circle, the space between us is healing, and the center of the circle is the place of integration. Angeles said that the placement of people in the circle was significant for *Four Fold Way*™ work. When working in a circle, pay attention to position:

- I sit in the place of the visionary, my own authenticity;
- The person directly across from me in a circle is a mirror of my inner teacher, and shows me what I'm learning about attachments and wisdom;
- The person to the right of me is my mirror for the warrior, teaching me about right use of power and leadership;

33

- The person to the left of me is my healer, teaching me about love.

Closing Well. Angeles always talked about closure and closing well at the end of a year-long program. When we close well, we have done honorable closure. If we do not close out a relationship or a life transition well, we may have regrets and may carry this baggage into our next experience. To begin well in something new, we must close well with the old experience. Completing and closing well opens the door for new opportunities to arise. In Buddhist teaching, the three heavenly messengers: death, illness, and old age make us prepare for closure. To the Mayans, the shedding skin serpent, and in Hawaiian cultures, the bursting sun are images that remind us to close well. The phrase "to enclose" means to put protective boundaries around our experience, and to bring a circle together (but it is never ending).

Four steps to honorable closure, or closing well in a group, ending a relationship, or at the end of a year are:

1. Express what I am grateful for about this group, experience, or year.
2. Acknowledge where I have been positively impacted.
3. Express how I have been challenged or grown.
4. Say what I need to say, or take an action to feel complete.

Co-Creating. Every relationship and collective is co-created. Relationships require mutual engagement and a consideration of a common good, not just the good of the self. When we stay in our hearts, the good we do is amplified, and so is our learning. We deepen our character. We also co-create problems in our relationships.

In terms of the greater world, Angeles noted in 2013 that the great diversity of cultures coming together because of travel and the internet means that we are in a time that allows people and ideas to come together in new ways. This sparks much creativity and two important things to consider are:

- What is the best way to anchor those who are consciously creating change? What tools are needed? What can best balance my inner and outer work?

- How can I increase my capacity to stay present and to take actions in the present to course-correct the past?

Collaboration. In my 2013 journal, Angeles recommended a book called *Opening Doors to Teamwork and Collaboration: Four keys that change everything (Katz & Miller, 2013).* She said that the four keys are:

1. Finding comfort in discomfort;
2. Listening as an ally;
3. Stating both one's intention and one's intensity to the collaboration; and
4. Sharing the street corner—knowing what the others are doing as well as sharing what I am doing.

Collage. Making a collage is a tool of integration. Use whatever images call to you. Angeles presented two different ways to interpret the completed collage.

1. Divide the collage into four quadrants:
   - What is in the upper right quadrant represents the mind.
   - The upper left quadrant represents the heart, emotions, and feelings.
   - The lower right is the spiritual and intuitive nature.
   - The lower left is the outer world of health, finances, work, and creativity.
   - The center is the place where I am unshakeable and in balance.
   - The quadrant with the most images wants to be used and is calling to manifest.

2. Ask yourself the following questions about your collage:
   - What is the largest image? That is what wants to be used and is the image of power.
   - What is the smallest image? This is what needs attention; what has been ignored.
   - What words are on the collage: these can be listed and repeated as affirmations or power words. Say them everyday to help manifest the ideas.

Collective Work. Angeles noted that the two major forms of collective work that we do is within family and work settings.

These settings both require us to show up and be present and to hold our own power. We can ask ourselves, "Do I show up differently in different contexts?"

In groups, we can only go as far as the weakest link-- anyone who consciously chooses not to participate/engage. Introverts often don't enter into dialogue for the first 4-6 weeks of collective work. This does not mean that they are not engaging; rather introverts tend to be slow processers and take more time to feel comfortable in group work. Introverts usually speak up in groups only when something has deep meaning for them. They are often intimidated by people who can express themselves easily and often.

Work in teams can only go as far as the work every individual team member is willing to do. What is the quality of connection to others that I bring to my collective work? What is my intention for speaking/sharing in a group? Does it create an opening for learning? Am I coming forward out of ego to impress, get attention, or from insufficiency? How can I be present-forward in my sharing in group? When do I offer excuses for bad behavior in the past? When I share stories from the past, the group work stalls. When someone is on the offense or defense, the work stalls and people will be resistant. We go on the offense or defense in groups when there are perceived threats around positionality, power, status, our relationship line, fairness, or conflict. How can I stay in the formidable middle and open?

In groups (consisting of 3 or more people), two processes occur simultaneously.

1. The primary process is what we see and observe. This includes the actual words spoken, the content of the message, and nonverbal cues.
2. The secondary process is the thoughts and feelings that arise because of the content and tone of the message. The speaker's message may affect the energy level of the group, cause others to time travel and take them out of the present. Alternatively, the speakers' content or tone may cause others to be reactive. If there is conflict, it needs to be cleared before the group disbands.

Comfort Zone. Angeles often used the analogy of the bird on its perch in a gilded cage, with all the water, food, and shiny objects it could ever want. The door is open, but the bird is afraid of leaving the comfort zone. It swings on its perch, tweeting away, closer and closer to the open door, but afraid to leave through the open door. Then, one day, the bird flies free into new, unknown territory. To truly learn something new or create, we have to leave our comfort zone. The open door is our growing edge. When we stay in the comfort zone, we are attached to not growing, and we are settling for less than we deserve. A question to ask myself is "Where am I being stretched at this time?" If we can explore that issue and stay with the discomfort, we may move out of our comfort zone and open ourselves to a breakthrough. Another way to consider our comfort zone is to ask "What am I tolerating because it's comfortable? Where am I afraid to confront my fears?"

Communication Skills. Angeles always talked about "tooling up" on skills, and the two she mentioned most often were communication and conflict. Communication is most effective when we make clear and direct requests and ask for what we need, rather than make others try to guess what that is. She warns us from the practice of expecting that our significant others or coworkers should know us well enough to be able to always know what we need. When we are unclear in our communications or expect others to be mind-readers, we foster chaos and disappointment. Tell the truth without blame or judgment; say what is so, when it's so (as long as the time and place are right); and do what you say you will do.

Compassion. One of the forms of love is compassion. The root word means "to suffer together" or to recognize another person's suffering and not blame or judge them for it. It can also be applied to our own behaviors. We need compassion for our own human foibles and have the capacity to forgive ourselves and move on.

Comparison. Comparing ourselves to others is always a dangerous game. Either we fall short and feel bad about ourselves, or we exceed the other and feel superior. We are each unique individuals with our own set of gifts and talents, and there is no need, and indeed, much potential harm, that comes from comparison.

Competition versus Cooperation. If we have an attitude of abundance rather than scarcity, we have no need to compete with others for goods, praise, status, or anything else. Communal societies learned that they can survive better and have more positive relationships with cooperation than competition.

Consistency. Consistency is another of the qualities that helps to build trust. When we say what is so, when it is so and do what we say we will we do, we are consistent, and therefore, become trustworthy. On the other hand, sometimes we consistently engage the same old destructive pattern, thinking each time that the result will be different. We must be open to change and recognize that we need consistency for our core values, but can give up unhealthy ways of being and doing that are not compatible with our life dreams and purpose.

Constricting. Fear is the big constrictor—it may constrict our hopes and dreams or make us hesitant to leave our comfort zone. Our personhood, as well as our current environment, becomes smaller when we could be larger and expand our world rather than constrict. When we do not recognize our sufficiency and wallow in pity, insecurity, or low self-esteem, we constrict our power.

Control. A sign of attachment is control. When we try to control circumstances or others, we are clinging to some fixed outcome. Control is usually triggered by fear, pride (needing to look good), or perfectionism. Control may stem from the irrational assumption that we can change someone else's behavior.

Courage. The root word in courage comes from "heart;" it takes heart to stand up and act in the face of fear. Courage does not mean having no fear; it means acting in spite of fear. A courageous person stands by their core, which is their heart. It does not involve armament, weapons, or defenses. If we name the fear, we can overcome it. Courage does not live in comparison or competition with others, but is tied to a deep authenticity unique to each person.

Course-correcting. Angeles frequently brought up the idea of course-correcting. Many of us have a fixed perspective and old habitual ways of responding, but Angeles noted that we can change our course (behavior, perspective) at every choice point. If we are getting off track or lapsing into old patterns, all we need to do is make another choice to correct our course. We have multiple opportunities every day to make different choices and change those old patterns, but to do that, we have to stay awake and recognize the choice points. Course-correcting can only take place in the present, but it can change our perspective on the past and create the opportunities for a better future.

Cradling Work. When feeling fear, we can soothe ourselves with certain behaviors that cradle us in our own self-love and presence: singing or chanting our name and the cradling posture are two methods. The cradling posture is holding yourself with your right hand on your heart and left on your belly (called the Chilton posture).

Creativity (as opposed to innovation). Angeles distinguished between these two. Innovation is tweaking what you are already know how to do, and can make into a new iteration; creativity is venturing into new and unknown territory to make something entirely new to you. Most of us innovate from the safety of our comfort zones. We delude ourselves into thinking that we are being creative.

Criticality. Angeles often asked "Is your sufficiency greater than your criticality?" That is, are you more positive than negative? Are you acknowledging all that is working in your life? Are you standing firm in your own strengths? Are you confident that you can handle any situation? Critical doubting voices within are the source of all violence, and one of the best things we can do for ourselves, and the world at large, is to monitor and hold in check our own self-critic.

Crucible. In alchemy, a crucible is a container in which the magic happens. In Angeles' teaching, any situation that allows learning and growth to occur was a crucible. She created circles of "important strangers" as her primary crucible for her teaching. A vision quest is another powerful crucible of learning.

Curiosity. Angeles was the most curious person I have ever met. She taught that approaching new situations, conflicts, or emotional challenges with curiosity opens the heart and mind to really listening to another perspective, or being open to possibilities. Curiosity trumps the doubting critical voices and staves off attachments. Another version of the saying above goes: "Is your curiosity greater than your criticality?"

The Cusp. The cusp is the time between seasons, where two archetypes overlap. It is a powerful time for change and breakthroughs. Between winter and spring, power and love combine. Between spring and summer, love and authenticity merge. Between summer and fall, we deal with the powerful combination of authenticity and letting go. Between fall and winter, the two resources are vision and power. Do I love my vision? Between fall and winter, we also are in a crux of letting go and power. What do I have the courage to let go of at this time?

What "C" words speak to you? What is your work at this time?

D is for Divine Discontent

I think the first time I heard Angeles use this term was when she reframed my story about my "midlife crisis." I felt restless and dissatisfied, though not overtly unhappy most of the time, and I felt impatient. I knew I needed some kind of change in my life, but I could not envision what it should be. I often had insomnia as my mind raced from place-to-place trying to land somewhere that felt more comfortable. I was nearing my 50th birthday, and thought to myself, "So this must be what a midlife crisis feels like." These feelings had started with my father's death, and intensified when my 45 year-old sister-in-law died unexpectedly. I was in a highly dysfunctional relationship and not feeling fulfilled by my work anymore. So there were many life transitions going on at once.

Then I met Angeles, just a month after turning 50, and she had a different explanation for those feelings. She said that whenever our spirit/soul needs us to change something about our lives, we feel the divine discontent or divine haunting, a restlessness and feeling of confusion about or inability to see our next steps. This distress motivates us to engage in a process of finding what has heart and meaning and aligning our lives with our dreams and values. This process of meaning-making can happen at any age, but is particularly common around the age of 50. Angeles said the decade of the 50s was a time to re-evaluate one's life and course-correct to align better with one's dreams and life purpose. So this divine discontent was right on schedule as I prepared to enter this contemplative decade.

The divine discontent can be found in the subtleties underneath our daily lives. When we pay attention, that drive is dissembling and unraveling our lives so that that it can be re-organized at a higher level. But we have to let go of the old so that the new can enter us. It's a time to ask ourselves, "What have I outgrown? What is calling to be released?" There is a process of discovery that takes some time—we have to gather information before we act. We can begin by clearing space for the new to come into our lives.

To address this divine discontent, we often must undergo a process of "soul retrieval," whereby we reclaim pieces of ourselves that we have given away in the past. We might give

41

away parts of our dreams, values, or integrity to appease powerful others like parents or bosses, to keep the peace in intimate relationships, or to be "successful" in ways that societal norms pressure us to be, rather than what our heart tells us. When the divine discontent arrives, it is the signal to start a process of re-aligning our lives with what has heart and meaning and reclaiming the authentic pieces of our being. We each have unique gifts and talents that we can offer to the world, but sometimes we are in relationships or jobs where we cannot manifest those gifts. It is hard to sort through the obligations, expectations, and demands placed on us by others, or absorbed through the media, and find our own true selves and desires.

Angeles used a variety of tools to access the "wisdom voice" or the clear, declarative voice within that knows what we should do. If we cannot hear the wisdom voice, we should not make decisions, but wait for clarity. Walking meditation in nature has been the most powerful tool for me to access the wisdom voice, which sounds suspiciously like Angeles' voice, using words from Angeles' teachings.

When the divine discontent appears at one's gate, it signals that we are in a transition. It is warning us to slow down, reflect, and let the wisdom voice emerge to tell us what we need. All the tools that Angeles taught of meditation (standing, lying, walking, sitting), journey work, or merely spending time alone and in silence in nature, are ways to access that wisdom voice. I have learned to sit with the discontent and wait for answers. When I was unable to sort through my distress about all the life transitions I was facing, I had the luxury to take a few months of leave of absence from my job, and live in San Francisco for a while to figure out if a move was right for me. I had the luxury of time to consider how to close out the other transitions so I could begin anew. When we align our lives to the authentic self and bring the inner and outer worlds into that alignment, the divine discontent goes away, at least until we face the next big transition phase.

Are you feeling the divine discontent at this time? If not, when in your life did you have that experience and what happened?

"D" Glossary

Daily Practice. Angeles, and other wisdom teachers, note that we need to have a daily practice of tracking, paying attention, and/or reflecting on our experience if we ever want to change. Daily practices keep us aware and engaged, and keep us from going back to sleep. She recommended many practices, so there is something that fits everyone's cultural backgrounds, personal preferences, and time frames. These include drumming, rattling, singing, chanting, giving gratitude, journaling, reflective reading, meditating, praying, pulling a Tarot card every morning, tracking certain qualities, using Spinoza's questions, and many others.

Daydreams. "The universe conspires to support the dreamer" (Paulo Coelho). In many indigenous cultures, there is a distinction between the kind of daydream that creates a desired future, and the kind that has potentially harmful effects on us, such as moving into comparison, fear, drama, or insufficiency. The "good" daydream is sealed with the phrase, "and that's a healing story," whereas the "negative" daydream elicits the comment, "and that's a story that doesn't need to happen." The daydream creates and we have a choice whether to give energy to the healing stories and life dreams, or to feed the negative dreams that leave us in pain and suffering. If our life is not as we want, we can "re-dream" it. We are also in our "living dream" the life in the present moment. Most of us do not stay present in our own lives for more than five minutes at a time. In one session, Angeles quoted Eleanor Roosevelt "Yesterday's a mystery, tomorrow's a mystery, today's a gift." Warrior work is a practice in staying present (awake) in our gift of life. That is, to be present in the living dream.

Death and Destiny. Another story that Angeles was fond of sharing was the idea that each day we walk with death at one shoulder and destiny at the other. Death asks, "Are you using the gift of life wisely?" and Destiny asks, "Are you doing what you were put here to do?"

Decade Assessment. In the *Second Half of Life* work (2010 journal), Angeles asked us to reflect on our experience by decade, noting at minimum, the gifts and talents, the primary challenges, and the important strangers of each decade. We can then note the seeds of learning from each decade and determine what we need to develop in our current decade. Make yourself a chart like the one below for this activity, going up to your current decade. This is not time to rehash old wounds and traumas, but to focus on what we learned from them (good and bad).

Angeles noted that a shift occurs for many people in the decade of their 50s, from focusing on family dreams and societal expectations to discovering and seeking one's own dreams. This leads to a high level of creativity in the 50s. This type of assessment can be used to track creativity or other qualities of personhood as well. Angeles also liked to encourage people to think about their youth, from about ages 10 to 14, and think about what we loved to do at that age. What did we do that caused us to lose track of time and that we did only because it brought us joy? These are activities or characteristics of ourselves that we can reclaim.

Decade	Gifts/Talents	Challenges	Important Strangers	Seeds of Learning
0-10				
11-20				
21-30				
31-40				
41-50				
51-60				
61-70				

Deep Listening. Listening is a rigorous practice, and rarely do we truly listen to others. We usually listen long enough to formulate a reply, or make an assumption. When people keep repeating the same story, it means that they do not feel heard. When someone listens deeply, they truly witness the other person. There are two things to listen for in any conversation: the content (primary process) and the thoughts, feelings, and memories the conversation elicits (the secondary process). In a group setting, this becomes more complex, because the content and feelings of the one talking can affect the other listeners in different ways. Highly emotional sharing may cause some group members to lean in and listen more deeply, and set others to time-traveling because it evokes painful memories, or checking out because it is hard to be present with another person's pain. But I can always track where I am myself in response to the other person's sharing.

Am I listening to reply, or listening to understand? Am I really listening or distracted by my own thoughts?

Deepening Work. This is one of the tracking questions that Angeles often asked her groups to do (along with softening, opening, and strengthening). Where do you have deepening work to do? What has deepened in your nature this season or this year? In *The Second Half of Life*, she discussed the need to address both ascending and descending aspects of our being. The descending, or deepening work, is to address parts of ourselves that we have neglected, such as the shadow sides of our accomplishments. They may be parts of ourselves that we have not claimed or reclaimed, or parts that we are not so proud of and would rather ignore or hide. Sometimes those are the qualities that we dislike or react to negatively in other people (they are mirrors for us). Angeles noted that some cross-cultural folk tales focus on the need to deepen by going down inside the self. The minotaur story, for example, urges the hero to "go forward; go down" into the caverns to find the beast (a disguised form of wisdom). The poet Gerald Manley Hopkins wrote about "the dearest freshest deep down things." These are our home or center, the qualities that matter most to us.

Destiny. Angeles always said that all humans are on this earth to love, be loved, and to create. Those are the universal destinies. We need to ask ourselves regularly, "Am I living the life I was put here to live?" "Am I using the gift of life well?"

Discernment. This concept helped me tremendously in figuring out the difference between being judgmental and noting some objective fact or common pattern in another. Judging is placing a value, either positive or negative, on some trait or behavior. Discerning is the objective noting of a behavior pattern or trait, without assigning any evaluative component to it. For example, we can note that a person has consistently not met deadlines, and is untrustworthy in this situation, without being judgmental about it. Discernment is being open without scrutiny, judgment or suspicion. It involves assessing right timing, placement, situation, and person, while staying in curiosity rather than criticality. Discernment practices involve asking myself questions:

- Is my response in the realm of my comfort zone, or a growth experience (most of us are afraid to step out of our comfort zone)?
- Do I have a "gut feeling" about the situation?
- Do I have clarity of mind, openness of heart, and is my gut aligned with my heart and mind?

Discipline. This word means "being a disciple unto one's self." That is, it involves applying a rigor to our daily practices and encounters that keeps us in our authenticity at all times. However, in my notes in 2008, I wrote that Angeles said that discipline without fire/passion is "duty" and may lead to resentment. We have to want to be disciplined or it won't be sustainable. Angeles asked us to consider "What gets in the way of my own rigor?" Where do I resist being disciplined? Discipline is a warrior practice.

Disturbance. Angeles describes this as a neutral word meaning that something in our lives has become unclear or is in the process of changing. It's a sign of movement and growth. However, if we get scared, we may try to control the situation and scurry back to our comfort zone. A question to ask when feeling disturbed is "What is making me feel reactive, irritable, or judgmental at this time?" These may be areas where I have patience work to do. Feeling disturbed is a signal to wake up and pay attention.

Dreams (night time). Dreams are gifts of preparation—they signal the work I need to do. If I cannot remember my dreams, it means I was taken for healing work. If I dream of my teacher, I need to access my own inner teacher. If I have a recurring dream, it has one of these three purposes (from Jung):

1. To get my attention,
2. To process losses,
3. To deliver important messages that often signal death/rebirth processes.

A few months after Angeles' death, just before a workshop on the continuation of her work led by Patrick O'Neill, I dreamed of Angeles. I was in the meeting room, seated in a circle of people with Patrick at the other side of the room. In one corner, I saw a small group of people talking, and I caught a glimpse of Angeles standing there. Overjoyed, I started to walk over to greet her, then the woman turned and it was not Angeles, and I heard the words, "Here and not here." What a powerful message to remind me that I have full access to Angeles as an ancestor, and I have the benefit from the ten years of teaching she left behind with me. She was reminding me to pay attention to my own inner teacher wisdom.

Drumming. In general, for many indigenous peoples' traditions, the drum is considered the imitation of the heartbeat. Angeles used shamanic drumming for journey work. This rapid rhythmic drumming helps people gain an altered state in a short period of time. The drum calls us back to ourselves, to our heart.

Dynamic Center. Dynamic energy is that which flows out of me to the outside world. What takes me out of my center? What draws me out of my authentic self? To explore these questions, I can track:

- When I get upset, I always _____.
- When I am faced with the unexpected, surprised, or thrown off balance, I _____.
- When I get afraid, I most often _____.
- I most often want to be seen as _____.
- I do not want to be seen as _____.
- The gift that I most use and stand behind is _____.

After considering each of these, I can identify which was the most difficult to address. These statements reveal habitual patterns of responding and show us where we have a tendency to lose our authenticity. Our initial reactions and feelings are normal, but we can learn to not indulge them, and to shift them so that they do not control us. In three steps to changing old patterns we can:

1. name it,
2. feel it, but don't indulge it,
3. take an action to change it.

Dynamism. This is one of three life forces (magnetism and integration are the others). It means to take initiative, to be proactive, organized, and capable of synthesis. It is associated with speaking, the sun, and in chanting in many religions, the sound "eeee." To chant them together, sing:

47

- "eeee" for dynamic;
- "oh" for magnetic (drawing energy to oneself, symbolized by the moon and associated with listening); and
- "ah" for integration (pulling together our learnings to create new patterns and new ways of understanding, symbolized by the stars).

When I am not living within my dynamic center, I can doubt my relationships.

What "D" words speak to you? What is your work at this time?

E is for Equanimity

I had heard this term, but never really understood it until working with Angeles. My background, in protestant, stoic Scandinavian stock, tended to the practical rather than the mystical. I was not exposed much to philosophy or Buddhist writing where I may have encountered the term. Yet, many people in my life lived it.

Equanimity, Angeles said, was "meeting a disturbance without causing a disturbance." This definition originally came from Patrick O'Neill, long-time co-teacher with Angeles. I have profound gratitude to both Angeles and Patrick for bringing this critically important quality to my attention, and modeling it so superbly.

In Buddhist traditions, equanimity is defined as an evenness of mind, a freedom from the ego, a state of equipoise that cannot be disturbed by gains or losses, praise or blame, or pleasures or pains.

That is, equanimity means not being ruled by desires, fears, doubts, and wants, but staying in a calm and balanced place of sufficiency even when the world around you is in chaos. It means to not allow the ego to get triggered by the other person or the circumstances. My parents were wonderful models of equanimity. My mother was known as "unshakeable" and my father as a kind and fair presence. Neither of them expressed intense emotion in either direction—negative or positive—but stayed in a comfortable middle zone most of the time, including times of crisis. I have so much gratitude to them both for modeling this behavior, that I have access to in times of need.

But this desirable trait also has a shadow side to it, at least in the stoic Midwestern variety that I learned. My father never expressed his feelings. He came home from work one day and announced that he had resigned from a job he had held for 25 years. My mother was caught completely unawares. When she asked him how long he had been unhappy at work, she was shocked to discover that he had been thinking of leaving the job for more than five years. She did not have a clue. My mother also had a shadow side of passive-aggressive behavior. As a teenager, sometimes I would come home to a stony silence and some banging of kitchen cabinet doors and know that she was upset with me, but sometimes I never knew why. She was a master of the silent treatment.

Because of my upbringing, I quickly become uncomfortable when my emotions swing to either extreme, and fall outside of that comfortable middle zone of calm and focused. Feelings like fear, anger, guilt, shame, and grief come over me, and I want to flee. I try to distract myself from them. A friend once told me that she had participated in a workshop where the facilitators guided them through a process of "feeling their feelings." The friend had felt much release of pain, both emotional and physical, after this process. For months, I puzzled over this. What would it be like to actually feel one's feelings? How do I release more than 60 years of social conditioning to not feel them? The idea makes me break out in a cold sweat. I think I fear that if I open those flood-gates, I will have 60+ years of emotion to deal with and it will be overwhelming. Fear of loss of control has ruled most of my life. I think I absorbed more of my mother's silent, tight-lipped determination to control her feelings than I would like to admit. I fear I also internalized too much of my father's tendency to bury his feelings from view.

So equanimity is both a gift I possess, and a challenge for me to continue to explore. There are times when I need to let myself feel more and learn to trust that I can handle it, whatever form the emotions take. I can be the one to change the unhealthy family dynamic that is related to the shadow side of equanimity.

What is your experience with the concept of equanimity?

"E" Glossary

Editing (and rehearsing). These are thought processes we engage in when we are out of our integrity. When we have to consider and revise what we say, or rehearse it, it often means that we are trying to please someone else, or maybe even be deceptive. We might be trying to fool others or ourselves. Angeles said that the wisdom voice is clear, simple, and unrehearsed. We might edit when we are "building a case" or trying to convince ourselves of something that goes against our core values or authentic self. We might edit to appease or get the approval of others. Sometimes we edit to avoid being vulnerable in a situation where we do not fully trust others, in ourselves, or the circumstances.

Ego. When our primitive needs and wants take center stage, we are controlled by our ego. The ego has all the narcissistic tendencies to focus only on myself, and operates in a survival mode. Angeles often talked of relegating the ego to the back seat and not letting it take the driver's seat. At other times, she would say, "if you let it in, keep it on the porch--don't let it trash your house." Ego tends to want power and status, and not things aligned with the heart.

Elements. The five elements are earth, air, fire, space, and water.

Embellishing. This happens when we get stuck in some old story or we are building a case. Each telling of the story elicits some responses from others—we bond with each over the terrible things that happen to us, or we get some attention or sympathy, and the story gets strengthened and expanded with the next telling. Angeles proposed that telling old painful stories to others in all their gory details is like backing up the garbage truck and dumping our waste on our friends. She recommended using therapists for the resolving of old stories, or telling them to a tree or rock so that we do not wear out our friends, and keep the old stories alive. Most of the time, those stories are not current, and much is working in our lives. The focus on what did not work in those old stories keeps us stuck and looping. If a story must be told, keep to the simple facts without embellishment, and focus on the lessons learned from the experience. Those lessons can help us from having the story repeat itself in the future, or have the old pain and suffering revisited with each new telling of the story.

Emotional Integrity. Angeles said that the mature way to respond to feelings is to acknowledge them without judgment. It is ok, even necessary, to feel them, and to acknowledge them in others as well. However, we should not indulge them or make decisions when in a highly emotional state. When reactive, we can say to others, "I'm angry, and not reliable now," or "I am very sad and not clear about this issue right now." We need to give ourselves time to process and not expose others to our reactivity. When we are responsible about managing our emotional reactivity, we are in emotional integrity.

Emotional Lumping. This is when we are too absolutist in our thinking, so that if someone is critical of us or does not agree with everything we say or believe, we think we cannot be friends or the relationship must end. Disagreements or negative feedback are perceived as a threat because we fear loss. Ironically, we often lose these relationships anyway because of our fear.

Empathic Joy. This is the highest state of consciousness. It holds no control, envy, jealousy, comparison, or competition. We are genuinely happy for the other person.

Empowerment. The warrior or leader in us holds the resource of power; power over or empowerment. Right use of power empowers others to stand on their own whereas power over can impact our relationships in harmful ways. I can ask myself, "How do I empower myself? Where/when do I give away my power? Who do I feel safe with? What qualities create safety?" These insights lead to empowerment of self and others.

Excellence. Angeles said we should strive for excellence; doing high quality work to the best of our ability at that particular time, rather than perfection. If we strive for perfection, we will fall short most of the time, because perfectionism does not tolerate mistakes. Excellence may result in mistakes, but we can frame them as "mis-steps" and learn much from them. Excellence allows us to take our learning to the next level. Perfectionism stops the learning process.

Expertise. Angeles defined this as developing a skill or talent, and then recycling or re-inventing it in new ways. It is not really creativity, just a re-packaging of what we already know. When we get stuck in expertise, we stop growing. Expertise is similar to innovation: staying within what is knowable and successful. In other words, when we are within our expertise, we are firmly within the territory of our comfort zone. If we want to keep growing as a person, we have to step out of the comfort zone and into the unknowable.

What "E" words speak to you? What is your work at this time?

F is for Forgiveness

Forgiveness is the act of giving up anger and resentment held over some past transgression. Three types of forgiveness work that are needed to stay within one's integrity are:

> 1) when I have wittingly or unwittingly harmed another person;
> 2) when another person has wittingly or unwittingly harmed me; and
> 3) when I have self-forgiveness work to do.

Earlier in life, I thought of forgiveness as an either/or situation: I have forgiven or I have not forgiven. But Angeles taught it as a process that occurs in typical cycles. First we forgive in the mind, then in the heart, and finally, in the belly, the seat of embodied wisdom. The first phase, in the mind, is often the stage of fire/rage, whereas the final stage of the body releasing the attachment comes with tears of release.

I have one long-standing grudge against a person that I have not been able to let go. I cannot yet bring myself to forgive this person for a wrong-doing that happened ten years ago. Every few months, I return to this issue, and wonder if I'm ready to forgive. I usually find myself re-hashing the old story and I get all riled up with righteous indignation again, and I cannot move to forgiveness. I fear that I have not completed even the first phase, because the fire is still there. Even now, writing about it, I feel the urge to tell you the story, to show how unfairly I was treated. I'm still firmly attached to the story, and convinced that any reasonable person would see how wronged I was by this person. It's a great story, as far as stories go: full of drama, clear-cut victims and villains, and plot turns and twists. I've built an air-tight case against this person in my mind.

What a relief it would be to forgive this wrong-doing. I can clearly see the harm my attachment to this resentment has done to me. The guilt of regret in how this situation turned out is still strong, and holding on to the old grudge keeps me out of my full sufficiency. What energy it takes to stay mad at myself or another person for past transgressions, energy that could be so much better directed to productive and creative work. The anger and resentment I feel hurts only me; it does not punish that other person in the least. I know this in my rational mind, but my heart and belly have not moved to forgiveness of the other person yet, so all I can do is forgive myself for not being ready. However, I know the issue will keep coming up for me periodically until it is resolved, and I think the reflection on this particular issue has pointed out a pattern for me. The situations that are hardest for me to let go are when I get triggered to believe an injustice has been done to me, or another. I get a sense of "righteous indignation."

This underlies a lot of the pain that I cause for myself, so I did a bit of research on the concept, which is sometimes called "moral indignation." Oscar Wilde called it "jealousy with a halo." It is an attitude of superiority and specialness. I feel it sometimes when I rebel against a change in my life that I know would make me feel healthier—even in regard to mundane things like when I needed to give up caffeine because of an effect it was having on me. I felt that upwelling of righteous indignation (and often a psychic and actual indigestion goes with it) and said to myself like a petulant child, "it's not fair!" This feeling triggers rebellion, anger, arrogance, and keeps me stuck in less than optimal ways of being.

Angeles said that at the end of life, there are only a few basic things that people want to hear. Among them is "I forgive you, " and "Please forgive me." Forgiveness is a major form of letting go. I truly hope that I have found a way to forgive this person before I reach the end of my life. But even more importantly, I need to recognize when I am triggered by this feeling of injustice, and do not indulge it. Maybe this particular attachment to resentment has attached to me like a barnacle and won't let go until I let go of my earthly body, but perhaps I can stop future resentments from growing so strong.

One night recently, when I could not fall asleep, I pulled a book from my shelf at random. It turned out to be Jack Kornfield's *The Art of Forgiveness, Lovingkindness, and Peace* (2002, Bantam Books). Kornfield noted that forgiveness work involves giving up on the idea that we can make the past better. The past is past. Sometimes I wonder if I hang on to this resentment because a part of me thinks that if I can prove this person to be the villain I have made her to be in my head, that the outcome of our conflict will change and a lost relationship will be restored. All the time-traveling in the world will not change the past, but I am stubbornly refusing to accept that fact.

An exercise that Angeles proposed to help with forgiveness work, is to journal or discuss these questions with a small group:

- What do I most want to be forgiven for at this time?
- What do I allow to get in the way of my forgiving others?

That second question really seems to capture the work I have to do on this issue. After ten years, why I am still indulging? Is this my rebellion? My hurt pride? My sense of betrayal and loss? It's time to identify those underlying factors that are getting in the way of forgiveness.

Where do you have forgiveness work to do?

"F" Glossary

False-Self System. Our conditioning from birth on from family, culture, teachers, and others often forces us to hide or edit our true selves in order to survive. The survival mechanisms result in creating an elaborate new self; but it's a false-self. Over time, we become so accustomed to the false-self, that we lose touch with our authentic selves. We need a process of soul-retrieval to restore our lost parts and cast out the false-self. Signs of the false-self are the masks we put on to hide ourselves, and when we edit, rehearse, appease, and seek approval from others. So who is the real me? Angeles was fond of this poem:

> *I am not I*
> *I am this one walking beside me whom I do not see,*
> *whom at times I manage to visit*
> *and whom at other times I forget;*
> *Who remains calm and silent while I talk*
> *and forgives, gently, when I hate.*
> *Who walks where I am not,*
> *who will still remain standing when I die.*
> *--Juan Ramon Jimenez*

Fair Witness. When we really listen to others and are able to hear their struggles and acknowledge their commitments, we are being a fair witness. We can do this for ourselves as well. We can listen to our inner struggles without blame or judgment, but with compassion and forgiveness. The fair witness reduces the influence of the self-critic.

Family. Angeles said that our family of origin conditioning often lasts until one is about 40 years old, when we become more aware of the family patterns and seek to change them. Parent and child bonds are the only appropriate place for unconditional love—this type of love is not for intimate relationships or close friendships; these require more limits and boundaries.

Fate. Angeles announced in 2003 that fate is "the intersection between choices and beliefs." We may use the concept of fate as a way to avoid responsibility. Our destiny is changeable.

Fear. Fears drive much of our undesirable behavior in the world. In the case of relationships with others, we may have fear of abandonment, fear of entrapment, or both. We may test our relationships out of fear, putting the relationship at jeopardy. Angeles always said that love must be freely given and never tested. Most fears are manufactured in the mind, and are not real threats to us. As Rumi said, "Don't move the way fear wants you to." Fear constricts energy and creativity, and triggers the critical, doubting voices.

One of my favorite of Angeles' expressions related to fears. When talking about some irrational fear, she would clasp her hands to her cheeks and say, "eeck, squeak, freak!" Bringing a sense of humor to the discussion of fears softens and makes it a little easier to talk about. To address fears, some of the questions Angeles asked us to explore were: Where am I experiencing fear at this time? Where am I experiencing doubt? A centering prayer/phrase that helps dispel fear and doubt is "This too shall pass." We can ask ourselves, "Where have I addressed fear and emerged fearless?"

Fire. There are many types of fire in Angeles' teaching that symbolize motivation and passion. The creative fire is the one that takes no wood. The fire of vision includes our life dreams and purpose. The heart's fire is our love nature. Finally, the soul's fire is the divine discontent and restlessness that prompts us to change and grow, and to learn who we are beyond our roles and identities.

Five Forces. These affect us every day, but become even more important in the second half of life.

- The Healing Force: The need for self-care and forgiveness work.
- The Creativity and Generative Force: the need to explore new things, and create. Also involves the "great shedding" or letting go of the things that no longer serve us to make room for the new.
- The Integrative Force: the need to put together all the experiences of our life and use the past for character building and to create a better future. This force uses the formidable middle to conserve energy and avoid drama.

- The Initiation Force: to stay in the role of learner, with curiosity and openness. It fosters a re-enchantment with the world, and a wish to be caught learning. This force looks for win-win collaborations rather than winning over.
- The Transformative Force: the flexibility to accept change. Water is a teacher of this: fluid and adaptable. Most of us want agreement and acknowledgement, not change. Transformation requires change beyond the comfort zone.

Flexible. "Be like bamboo, strong but yielding, " Angeles would say. Water is also a symbol of flexibility, as it is able to change its course around obstacles and keep moving. Being inflexible is another sign of attachment. We can assess our flexibility by paying attention to how we respond to surprises and the unexpected. Sometimes we deceive ourselves and use flexibility as a cover-up for appeasement—that is, we rationalize our appeasement as just being flexible. We need discernment to make the distinction.

Flooding. This is when emotions are out of balance and cloud our judgment. When in this state, we are unable to take right action or even name the emotion without fear. When in this reactive state, it is helpful to remember that "action absorbs anxiety," and take one small step toward restoring balance. Anything that grounds or centers us may help to reduce the feeling of being flooded with emotion.

The Fog Machine. Sometimes we pretend to be confused when we are really not in order to avoid addressing some issue or taking some action that is hard. Instead, we take the weak-hearted approach and turn on the fog machine. Angeles also referred to this as "manufactured confusion."

The Formidable Middle. There is an indigenous notion of the middle way; the path that is between the extremes, that stays true to your authenticity and does not take you too far off that path. Staying in equanimity keeps us on the middle path, between drama and collapse.

Four Fold Way™. This is the name that Angeles gave to her main teachings: the way of the Warrior, Healer, Visionary, and Teacher. This program was developed from cross-cultural research on the perennial wisdom accumulated by indigenous cultures from around the world, pulling the methods/tools of achieving a life of integrity. Most other "wisdom texts" in our culture come from western cultures rather than indigenous traditions.

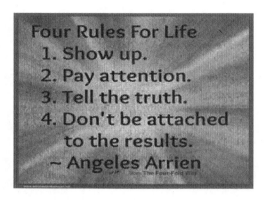

Four Forces. At any time, we can assess how we are using the four forces of life.

1. Love: What am I learning about love at this time? Who are my teachers of love?
2. Death: Am I using the gift of life well? How do I deal with loss?
3. Power: Where am I in terms of my energy, vitality, strength, and stamina? Am I using my power wisely and not giving it away?
4. Time: Am I spending time at nature's rhythm? Do I use time wisely? Am I obsessed about time? Do I limit my potential by telling myself stories that I don't have enough time? Time is a figment of our mind, used to impose order on the world. In my 2012 journal, Angeles noted that different cultures have different interpretations of time. In Basque tradition, time tracks to the mountains and day time versus night-time. In some cultures, time is "polymorphic" meaning that a person can show up at any time to honor an event, unlike in our western world when an event has a set beginning and end. Healing takes place in nature's time, which is slow to medium.

Four Quadrants. Angeles often gave us an activity that involved dividing a piece of paper into four sections, labeled work, relationships, health, and finances. She asked us to consider what our work was in each area. In the center of the diagram lies our personal growth or character development work. Here is an example of an alternative tracking tool that could be used for this activity. Once you consider your responses, you could ask "Am I over-identified in any quadrant?" "Am I balanced?" You can look for patterns that recur in more than one quadrant that might signal the need for character development work.

Quadrant	What's working	What's challenging
Work		
Finances		
Relationships		
Health		
My character development		

Four Ways of Seeing. For any problem in your life, consider it using these four questions:

1. What does your intuition tell you?
2. What is your perception of the problem?
3. What insight do you have?
4. What is your vision for this problem—what is the big picture? That is, look beyond the specific problem to see if it represents a pattern in your life.

What "F" words speak to you? What is your work at this time?

G is for Gratitude

"Gratitude keeps the heart open," Angeles would say. Gratitude keeps us in the present, keeps our relationships current and acknowledged, and helps us to integrate our experiences. To know for what one is grateful, is to know what we are learning from life.

A practice that Angeles recommended was to give gratitude every day in four different ways. We can give thanks for:

The **blessings** in our lives. These are things, experiences, and people that bring us joy. I find this one the easiest. I can point to having a job that I love, having wonderful and supportive friends, living in a place with an abundance of natural beauty, never having to shovel snow, and having a loving and kind partner. Blessings are usually obvious.

The **learnings**—the seeds of wisdom we acquire through life experience. These show where we are growing. Even if they are hard and painful experiences, we can be grateful for what we learn about ourselves. For example, I am grateful for being present with my mother when she died. It was an excruciating and painful experience and many times I wanted to escape. In the end I am so grateful that I was able to witness her passing and stand by her in the biggest letting go process of our human experience. I learned much about myself. But in a typical day, it is a bit harder to answer this question. What did I learn today? One has to be fully present and paying attention to the small daily lessons to be able to acknowledge them. This takes rigorous tracking. In addition, as Oscar Wilde said, experience is the hardest teacher because it gives the test first, and then the lesson. We have to be paying attention to get the lesson.

The **mercies**—these are the kindnesses extended to us by others; who treated me with compassion today? Who helped me with some life challenge? Who was kind to me when I was frazzled or worried about something? Who extended forgiveness to me? Rumi said "Suffering is a treasure, for it conceals mercies." What have the traumatic or stressful experiences of the day taught me? Who came forward to offer help? What did I learn about myself?

The **protections**—what things/people kept me safe today? Where did I feel protected? We often take these for granted. I can be grateful that I live in a safe neighborhood with adequate shelter, food, clothing, and have all my material needs met. I am protected by the wide array of workers in my community: law enforcement, fire fighters, the people who test the water quality, the ones who clean the streets and haul away my garbage. I am protected by the farm workers who plant and harvest the food that I eat. My work life is supported by the janitors, cooks, barristas, textbook writers, student advisors, and many staff members whose invisible work allow me the time and freedom to do my job. I live in San Francisco, and many nights I can hear the foghorns blowing in the bay—the sound reminds me of the protections all around me. All these unseen protections need acknowledgment.

Grateful seeing is a practice of recognizing that the good, true, and beautiful is greater than the problems or dissatisfactions of life. The good we do in our lives is more valued and remembered than our errors or mistakes. Grateful seeing is the ability to look first at what is working, without minimizing the challenges or hardships of our lives. Usually, much more is working in our lives than is not working, yet we tend to focus on the parts not working. If we start with some gratitude for what is working, we are better able to address those smaller concerns in areas that are not working as well. Gratitude increases our capacity to care, and enhances our compassion, justice, honesty, and respect for others and the world we live in. Some of the obstacles to gratitude are greed, ambition, pride, anger, fear, and envy.

Angeles pointed out research showing that a 5:1 ratio of gratitude to complaint predicts high chance of success in relationships, and in work settings predicts greater productivity. She also said that it takes three positive thoughts or comments to negate one negative thought/comment. If we make gratitude a daily practice, we can increase the positive side of this ratio and keep negativity at bay. This reminded me of something a speaker at a workshop on gratitude once said: positive comments are like Teflon—they tend to slip away quickly. Negative comments are like Velcro—they stick to us indefinitely.

Using Angeles' four types of gratitude forces one to go deeper with a gratitude practice, and access inner wisdom in a way that merely stating or writing about what one is grateful for in general, does not. I have noticed from experience that the usual gratitude journal that merely counts one's blessings does not force me to dig deeper.

I found this magnet in a bookshop on the Oregon coast while working on this book. It seemed so relevant because this process of reviewing my journals has forced me to acknowledge how often I was lying to myself without even knowing it. My journals are peppered with pretty delusions and rationalizations, and it took me time to reflect on them before I recognized them as self-deceptions. I am deeply grateful that my life affords me opportunities for solitary reflection so that I can recognize those "beautiful lies" and course-correct.

How do you practice gratitude in your life? With the people who are most important to you, what is the ratio of gratitude (respect, acknowledgment) to complaints or criticisms?

"G" Glossary

Gandhi's 7 Blunders. These are also known as the Seven Social Sins. In my 2012 journal, I found reference to this list. When Gandhi was near the end of his life, he gave his son this list of mistakes or mis-placed priorities. They can be used to evaluate one's current life. The seven are:

1. Wealth without work
2. Pleasure without conscience
3. Knowledge without character
4. Politics without principles
5. Commerce without morality
6. Science without humanity
7. Worship without sacrifice

Gate. Angeles often used the symbol of the gate. She would say, "whatever is at your gate, you can handle it, otherwise it wouldn't be there." Other times she would say about doubting or critical voices, "they can come to the gate, but you won't let them trash your house." The gate is a threshold between worlds: the inner and outer world or the known and the unknown. Our inner critical voice makes us doubt our ability to handle whatever comes our way, but we have all the resources we need.

Generative Speaking. One of the things that really helped me in my own work, both personal and professional, was the idea of generative speaking. Angeles taught this process in her mentor groups. She wanted us (and she modeled) speaking in groups in a way that moved the process forward in a positive way. A generative comment is one that asks a genuine question, provides seeds of learning, or asks for guidance on an issue (not a story). It does not preach/teach, seek attention, or focus on insufficiency (poor me). The whole concept of "seeding" was critical to success of Angeles' groups. If a member lapsed into a sad old story, people lost interest after a while, especially if they had heard this story before. But if a member gave just enough context: "I have an old pattern of competition with my sister," and then the sharing was about how that pattern was shifted, everyone could learn from it. Sharing in the group was most productive when it was "present-forward" or an issue that was being considered in the present (not rehashing the past) that could lead to an action to change the future. I believe this process is what made Angeles' groups so productive, and kept them from becoming too much like therapy sessions.

Generosity. Another attribute of a loving nature is generosity. Being generous with one's time and attention is a gift to others. Generosity is an expression of true giving and receiving with no ulterior motives—no pity, no arrogance, no expectation of something in return. Angeles often recommended that we practice anonymous acts of kindness to foster a generous spirit.

Genuine. This is another word for authentic, being one's self. Also, genuine is in contrast to insincere. A genuine apology is one that includes being sorry and taking action not to repeat the behaviors; genuine forgiveness is truly letting go and releasing the self or other from blame, not an appeasing or trying to smooth over a conflict without actually making any changes in behavior.

Giving Myself Away. We learn from an early age that other people, more powerful than us, people we depend on, have expectations for us. Most of us begin to give away pieces of ourselves in childhood, so that by adulthood, we have lost touch with our essential nature. As adults we may continue patterns of appeasement that give away our power, or let people violate our boundaries. We may do this in family, in intimate relationships, at work, or with friends. Each piece that we give away takes us farther away from our authentic nature. To give pieces of ourselves away in adulthood is to take a victim role.

Grace. When things come to us with ease, we describe the situation as grace. In grace, there is no separation between self and the world and everything feels right, just as it is. Grace has a simple elegance; an economy of motion. In the Christian tradition, grace also refers to being in God's favor. There are four qualities of grace:

- Courage to stand by my heart
- Trust
- Flexibility
- Patience/Humility

In another session, I wrote that the four graces are compassion, loving-kindness, joy, and equanimity.

Grounding. This term is similar to centering, to rooting ourselves in the earth and our own sufficiency to keep us strong and focused. Angeles asked the mentors to do a grounding meditation before groups to create a sacred space within the room (and within us as anchors). She recommended that we visualize a light that connects us all at the belly, the heart, and the head in a circle, and then arches over the top of the circle to the other side. Other ways of grounding are to feel one's feet solidly on the floor or the earth and imagine that we are sending down roots. Her saying about "our long tall bodies and our deep deep roots" was a visual image for that grounding. Being firmly grounded gives us the safety to stretch and expand.

Growing Edge. This is the area just beyond our comfort zone, where we are able to stretch ourselves into new territory, or express our creativity in novel ways. The growing edge is always a little bit scary, as it lies on the boundary of the unknown.

Guilt. Guilt is a control strategy when applied to others, and a paralyzing agent when internal self-blaming stems from guilt. Guilt feeds off of low self-esteem. It is an indulgence, because if I let myself wallow in guilt, I believe that I have disappointed myself or others, and have no desire or motivation to change. Guilt is a major tool of the inner critic.

What "G" words speak to you? What is your work at this time?

H is for Heart

"Listen with the deep ear in the chest" --Rumi

So much of Angeles' teachings were about the heart. Her archetype of the healer was all about the four chambered heart, finding what has heart and meaning in life, and aligning ones' values and activities around it. The heart is about love, engagement, commitment, and healing; it is the portal to the soul. It is being clear about what has meaning for us, and thus, is aligned with our core values and life dream. When we are not clear, and are confused, we can create chaos around us, and sometimes seek attention from others in an attempt to get them to solve our problems for us. We do not always take responsibility for our own healing. We can take the mature path and track what is healing in our lives—what people, places, and activities promote healing? Questions to promote healing are:

- Do I have forgiveness work to do?
- Am I doing anything that gets in the way of my loving myself or loving others?
- What is being renewed in my nature at this time?
- Where is there joy, abundance, and generosity in my life?
- Where am I shutting down or feel I am not deserving?
- Love is the ultimate healing force; where do I love myself? Where do I have self-inflicted wounds and martyrdom?

A tool or gift of the healer is the ability to ask questions that help self and others find solutions to life challenges. Instead of giving advice, the healer asks probing questions that help others get to the heart of the matter, so to speak.

It was during healer work in Angeles' group that she first introduced the idea of writing haiku. She said that poetry bridges the language of the heart with our outer experience. Haiku is uniquely suited to doing Angeles' work because it so succinctly captures the heart of the learning, using a nature metaphor. It is a great container for seeds of learning.

A haiku has three lines. The first and third lines have five syllables and the second line has seven. It must include a nature metaphor.

Once Angeles noted, "My life is like a haiku. Within my limitations, I have endless possibilities."

Angeles also noted that healing is a process-- sometimes a very long one. My old journals were full of one old story of loss, betrayal, and of regrets. I have dozens of examples of attempts to let go of this story. The journals recorded my anguish at the return of the old feelings in spite of these multiple letting go rituals. I tried writing the story in a letter to the person I lost and then burying it under a tree. Once I wrote the letter and burned it. I told the story to a great boulder, and another time, I pitched it into the ocean on a prayer arrow asking to be released of the story. I stopped sharing the story with others, hoping that it would dissipate. For some reason, I'm still getting something out of this story, or I would have released it long ago.

Even now, ten years later, sometimes the pain of the loss is acute. The lesson, for me, is a recognition that a process sometimes is never fully complete in one's lifetime. The grief transforms slowly into a familiar old memory, but it no longer drives one's actions after a time. The phrase "forgive and forget" is a misnomer. It is far better to forgive, but remember. If a betrayal occurred or a mistake was made, we don't want to repeat it. Heart connections can never be severed, but their form may change. We may still love someone, but cannot be with them.

One particular question explored in groups of three in a FourFold Way session sparked deep responses from my group: "What feedback am I consistently getting that I choose to ignore?" The follow-up question was "What's keeping me from receiving this feedback and changing?" What's the pay value of ignoring the feedback and remaining in the status quo? We cannot heal if we hold on to the stories of the past—they close the heart down.

Here is an activity to assess the condition of your heart related to current challenges. The definition of the negative side of each chamber of the heart is in each box, because it is easier to understand and explain in words than the positive side. Start by thinking of a current issue that is challenging you, or where you feel stuck. Consider the state of the four-chambered heart in regards to this issue. Give a piece of evidence of your status in each chamber.

Am I open hearted or closed (am I holding on to grudges, am I showing up and being present, do I have an expectation for how this situation should be)?	Am I full-hearted or half-hearted (needing to release or re-negotiate, not being fully present)?
Am I strong-hearted or weak-hearted (appeasing, avoiding, giving my power away, or have unresolved conflicts with another person)?	Am I clear-hearted or doubting (engaging in self-criticism, confusion, second-guessing: Second guessing comes from the mind, not the heart)?

Where do you need to focus your work to get unstuck? Is it an issue of one chamber, or more than one?

Another way to use the four-chambered heart for reflection is to ask yourself: Where in my life am I currently full-hearted? Where am I strong-hearted? Where am I open-hearted? In what circumstances am I clear hearted? These show what is working, and where I have work to do.

Angeles said that three medicines of the heart/healings are genuine acknowledgment, apology, and laughter. I started writing humorous stories about past stories of pain and loss, and these were healing for me. If I could laugh about it, I was no longer attached to the suffering. The word heart contains ear, earth, hate, art, and hear. "The art of hearing is to hear the earth to transform hate." A heart meditation that Angeles taught (2009) was:

> Place your left hand on your heart, and your right hand on top of the left. Focus on your breathing and your heart beat until the two align. Now visualize a fire around your heart, burning out anything that is false or toxic.

In 2005, in a session about manifestation, Angeles said that the heart, mind, and will need to work together to produce purposeful action. The heart produces the "what" (what has heart and meaning, what is my vision). The mind produces the "how," the step-by-step process needed to manifest the vision, and the will provides the "when," or the intent to stay with the process until the vision is manifest.

All the archetypes need the resources of the others, but love and keeping the heart open to receive life's lessons and blessings may be the most important resource of all. Without an open heart, we are unwilling and unable to keep growing as individuals and in our relationships.

What heart work most resonates with you and why? Where do you need healing work at this time?

"H" Glossary

Healing. The healer archetype is all about self-care as well as promoting healing in others. Sometimes the shadow side of healing is to give yourself away to others and not engage in adequate self-care. Angeles always pointed out that the Dalai Lama was thought to say, "me first, then you, with love." We are no good to others if we do not take care of ourselves first. We can ask ourselves, "What is calling to be healed in my nature at this time?" People who are healing agents are funny, joyful, have a relaxing presence, are kind, curious and see us as we really are. Who are the healers in my life at this time? What is the healing that I am avoiding? Have I placed myself well at work and within relationships? The portals of healing include beauty, order, color, joy and laughter, and silence. Love is the greatest of the healing forces. People who are healers can be seduced by the need to be needed (this is one of their shadows).

Helper Allies. Angeles had a number of different things to say about helper allies; the animal creatures that are meaningful or keep appearing in our lives. They bring us messages about ourselves (Angeles referred us to the interpretations in Ted Andrew's *Animal Spirits*). Appreciation of the animals is a way of extending gratitude to mother earth. After a vision quest, Angeles would spend much time discussing the animal visitations and what they meant.

In my 2012 journal, I found a group activity that Angeles had us do around the helper allies of the warrior. In groups of 5, each person was assigned one of the following helper allies to embody. Each animal had a lesson about leadership and power:

- Bear: the bear protects family and community, is territorial, and sets good boundaries. Bear also symbolizes hibernation: a period of reflection, introspection, and deep healing.
- Eagle: the eagle symbolizes vision, perspective, attention to detail, and trusting one's own vision. Eagle sees the whole as well as the parts.
- Mountain lion: Lions are skilled at tracking, conservation of energy, trust in instincts, and going after what they want. They are fully awake and aware.

- Dolphin: Dolphin symbolizes interspecies communication, fluidity and flexibility. They are the warriors of the sea. They have acute hearing and incredible resilience.
- Turtle: Turtle models resourcefulness and protection of the earth as well as manifestation, trust, and integration of internal and external experience. Turtles are a symbol of the death/rebirth cycle.

The first person shared an issue that was currently challenging them, and then each other person offered some guidance that comes from the perspective of the helper ally they were assigned. Then the second person shared an issue and got guidance from the group, continuing until each group member had shared their challenge and all had given and received guidance from the helper ally perspective.

Hope. Once Angeles shared a story about political leader Vaclav Havel, who was asked if he was an optimist or a pessimistic. He gave the notion some thought, and replied that he was neither; instead he had hope. Hope is an expectation that things will unfold as they should. Hope is the antidote to apathy, fear, and cynicism. We can ask, "Where am I hopeful?" This shows where I have trust. Or as Emily Dickinson said:

> *"Hope is the thing with feathers*
> *That perches in the soul*
> *And sings the tune without the words*
> *And never stops at all."*

Humility. I don't recall Angeles talking about humility much using that word, yet she was the model of humility in her own way of teaching and being. She never engaged in comparison or expressed in any way in words or behavior that she felt superior to any person or living being. She focused on staying in her power and sufficiency. Her teaching focused on knowing that you have the resources to deal with any situation in which you find yourself. Some people may think of this as self-confidence, and in our society that is sometimes falsely labeled as arrogance or lack of humility.

Humor. Angeles always said, "Where you have lost your sense of humor, shows where you are attached." Her humor was gentle; never at the expense of another. Tracking loss of sense of humor

73

shows where you have forgiveness work to do. In 2005, Angeles said, "humor illuminates deeper truth through joy." She also liked to quote Victor Borge: "Laughter is the shortest distance between two people."

What "H" words speak to you? What is your work at this time?

I is for "Isn't it Interesting?"

Once in a golden hour
I cast to the earth a seed.
Up came a flower
The people said, a weed.
--Alfred Lord Tennyson

Often, when someone brought up a challenging issue in their lives, Angeles would say, "Isn't it interesting that..." And she would follow that phrase with an insightful analysis of the problem or pose a question for the individual. Instead of imposing a judgment on what the person said, as I was probably doing in my head, labeling the issue as stupid, petty, outrageous, naïve, sad, or whatever, Angeles always started with the neutral, "Isn't it interesting." This seemed to open up the other person to consider alternatives, and not get defensive.

Angeles always modeled curiosity, and noted that curiosity keeps the heart and mind open, rather than closed and fixed on a particular outcome. I think this curiosity and framing of questions with this phrase, "isn't it interesting" led the other person to consider the issue from a non-judgmental perspective. Or as Socrates said, "Wonder is the beginning of wisdom." Angeles was a wizard at helping people find solutions or new perspectives through asking them questions, rather than giving advice or telling others what she thought about the specific situation. Instead, she broadened the discussion to universal human conditions that most people could relate to. She was able to show us the various perceptions that people might have about any issue, like the difference in perceiving a flower versus a weed in Tennyson's poem.

This skill of guiding others to their own conclusions through questions requires deep listening and staying present to the conversation. As Stephen Covey once said, most people listen to reply, not to understand. We jump to an assumption within the first few minutes of conversation, and our curiosity is then satisfied because we think we have the answer. Staying in curiosity until the speaker is done speaking is a skill that few of us possess, but might help us to avoid judgments and mistaken assumptions, and lead to greater understanding of the person's situation.

I am a slow processor and I find the development of this skill in asking insightful questions in the moment to be especially challenging. I admire those who can come up with questions that foster that deeper thinking or reconsideration of one's position or perspective. What a gift! Many an evening I had the experience of thinking of just the right question as I was driving home from a session—an hour or so too late! Perhaps if I had been listening more closely in the first place, those questions would have come up sooner. Deep listening with curiosity rather than judgment or criticality is a skill that I need to "tool-up" on.

What is the state of your own curiosity at this time?

"I" Glossary

Illness as Initiation. In my 2009 journal, there is a section about illness as a state of being out of balance. The initiation process that restores balance has three phases:

1. surrendering and honoring the new limits of the body.
2. courage to overcome denial and accept the new limits (but recognizing we still have unlimited creativity). Angeles noted that when we feel better, we often push those limits and may experience relapse.
3. The body commits to wholeness and will conserve energy by pacing itself. We have to get over our identification with strength, vitality, athleticism, and other qualities that are no longer in our repertoire.

Illusions. Angeles pointed out two major illusions (or delusions) most people have that cause much suffering:

- Relationships are for the purpose of making me happy. In reality, I am the only one responsible for my own happiness.
- I have the power to change someone else. In reality, I can only change myself, but if I do that, my relationships with others will change as well.

One of the reasons that Angeles liked the Spinoza questions so much, was because they ask us to consider what makes us happy that is not relational—the question makes us consider how we make ourselves happy or unhappy. She was fond of pointing out that if happiness came from other people, that happiness was "frosting," not the cake.

Important Strangers. Angeles pointed out that certain people come into our lives to help us with certain issues; maybe we need to be shaken awake, maybe we need to fall in love, maybe it's just something a stranger says in passing that has tremendous impact. When we are in a workshop, we may benefit greatly from something a stranger says. That person may stay in our lives for an hour, or a day, a year, and maybe even become a lifelong friend eventually. Angeles would also say that in any group, whoever shows up is just the right medicine that we need at that time.

Independence/interdependence. Many people highly value their independence, sometimes to the detriment of their significant others and communities. In reality, we are interdependent and need each other to survive and to thrive. With family and significant others, establishing healthy limits and boundaries help us to keep our individual selves intact, but able to ask for help when we need it.

Indian Summer. This season is during the cusp between visionary and teacher work (August 21 to September 21), and is the most potent time to make changes. It is a time of unexpected blessings and opportunities. Angeles encourages us to consider "What are the possibilities that I have not yet considered?" "Where has there been flow and movement this summer?" Indian summer is the time to take action. What did I let lapse or ignore? What didn't I finish? I have another chance to address them now or let go of them.

Indigenous Wisdom. Angeles' big contribution to the world was compiling indigenous perennial wisdom. Others have focused only on the perennial wisdom texts and teachings that come from the western and European world. Angeles recognized the deep wisdom that cuts across all indigenous traditions, and that has relevance to all of us. This embodied cross-cultural wisdom way underlies the Four Fold Way ™.

Indulging. When we allow ourselves to wallow in our insufficiencies--in self-pity, judgment, blame, feeling superior or other "less than becoming" behaviors--we are indulging. Indulgence is a barrier to learning, and we can indulge by sharing an old painful story or staying too long in a state of insufficiency. Indulging can be a tactic to avoid taking an action. We use indulging to hedge our bets, buy more time, build a victim stance, hide our insufficiencies, or hide fear. Indulging is remaining in a past story of trauma that holds us back. We can take three steps to acknowledge past traumas and move past them:

- Acknowledge that yes, this happened to me and name it without drama or collapse.
- Reflect on what we learned from the experience (seeds).
- Express what we are grateful for about the experience (gratitude cracks the heart open and allows for healing).

Individuation. This is the process of separation from another. We first do it in childhood as we separate from parents, but also individuate with partners, when we come into our own sufficiency. Partners grow at different rates, and one's individuation process can cause distress for the other if they do not recognize it as a normal process.

Initiation. This is the capacity to birth something new, or create a marriage of parts inside of us that have been waiting to come together, or accomplish a letting go (sacrifice) of something old that did not serve us well. Initiations help us let go of three attachments:

- To self-importance (ego). This is my need to be "special" or to be seen in a certain way, a need for agreement or attention, or a need to be right. Who am I beyond my roles and identities? Self-importance comes from pride and arrogance.
- To the need to control, dominate, or manipulate others. Control is the opposite of trust. When I control, I strategize, appease, manipulate, or hide my true thoughts.
- To our body and possessions. This can include my body image as well as the physical body. There is freedom to giving up possessions.

Vision quests are a major initiatory crucible, but any type of healing/learning circle can do the same. Many of us enter our comfort zone instead of fully committing to change when in an initiatory crucible.

Inside Job. When referring to work that is our own personal responsibility, Angeles often said, "It's an inside job." No one else can do the work for us, nor can we do someone else's internal work for them. All of Angeles' programs focused on inner work. She noted that Rumi said "Work in the invisible world at least as hard as you do in the visible." Another quote she often used for inner work came from Emerson: "What lies behind us and what lies before us are small matters compared to what lies within us."

Insight. An insight is a new way of looking at something. It often comes as a result of reflection or taking time to reconnect with nature, allowing the inner wisdom voice to emerge. A Japanese saying highlights the importance of coupling insight with action:

Insight without action is a daydream
Action without insight is a nightmare.

Instinct Injured. Angeles used this term to refer to a state that occurs when we have been betrayed or deeply hurt, and therefore no longer paying attention to our intuition. Then we start to "normalize the abnormal" and exist in an unnatural state. For example, we may believe another person's efforts to control us are an sign of their love, thus normalizing control and manipulation. We can also do the opposite, and "abnormalize the normal." For example, we may start thinking that peace and harmony are boring and thus, abnormal, and feel a need to stir up some drama.

Insufficiency. This is a state of not standing within my own gifts and talents (sufficiency). Most cases of insufficiency are triggered by one of two things: fear or unhealthy pride (the need to be right or look good). We know we are not in our full sufficiency if we engage in comparing, competing, measuring, analyzing, judging, excessively processing, looping, or blaming.

Integration. Reflection and insights are only useful if they get integrated, so that we learn from our mistakes as well as from what's working in our lives. When we integrate our experience, we make different choices in the future. At the end of a vision quest, or the end of year or season, Angeles would encourage doing a creative activity that solidified the learning and lent itself to integration, such as a collage or other creative project. That which is not integrated will repeat itself until such time that it does get integrated.

Jung said that symbols will appear that signal the need to integrate—watch for the repeating symbols that indicate we are ready to integrate some learning. Integration work builds character and personhood. The photo that follows integrated some of the lessons from a vision quest—this is the view I had from my campsite and I saw lessons in the sky, the fog, the trees, and everything within my sight lent itself to a greater vision. Nature gives us many powerful symbols that we can use to learn about our own lives.

PAY ATTENTION

STAY ROOTED

STAY COOL IN EQUANIMITY

LOOK FOR THE BIG PICTURE

PRACTICE DISCERNMENT

GIVE GRATITUDE

STAY FLEXIBLE: GIVE BUT DON'T BREAK

WATCH THE LIGHT CHANGE AND ADAPT

VISION QUEST LESSONS 2013

Integrity. Integrity comes from the Latin, "untouched," in the sense of not being attached. The dictionary definition is:

> 1. adherence to moral and ethical principles; soundness of moral character; honesty.
> 2. the state of being whole, entire, or undiminished.
> 3. a sound, unimpaired, or perfect condition.

I think Angeles would most resonate with a combination of the first two: being fully sufficient (undiminished) and sound in our personhood (moral character). When we are in our integrity, we act from our core values and principles and pay attention to what has heart and meaning. "I commit with the integrity of my blood" is one of the sacred vows that Angeles suggested when we want to forge a break-through. These words were uttered through rituals like tobacco traps, medicine bags, or prayer arrows. If we have integrity, we say what we mean. The shadow side of integrity is self-deception (2008 notes). Angeles said that you can tell when a person is speaking from integrity, because they are clear and concise. They get to the heart of the matter quickly without a lot of excess words. The person with integrity speaks the truth at the right time and place. Everything is in alignment (heart, head, and belly) and they command respect.

Intention (sacred intention). An intention is a commitment to follow through and do what you want to accomplish in your life. A sacred intention is a promise to make good on your desired actions. It is important to set intentions everyday, asking for the resource that would best support the achievement of this intention, and then take a life-affirming action.

Interdependence. Although our western world tends to over value independence, interdependence is the way of nature. Fierce independence and clinging are unhealthy extremes while interdependence is the middle path that creates. Interdependence is mutual.

Intimacy. Angeles broke down this word as: **Into me see.** Intimacy is facing the fear of vulnerability to allow others to see you in all of your gifts, talents, fears, and human condition. To be intimate, you have to let go of the false-self. Five factors that increase intimacy in any relationship are honesty, trust, curiosity, respect, and vulnerability (sharing one's authentic self without drama or collapse).

Intuition. This is one of the four ways of seeing, and involves accessing the inner wisdom voice. This voice is the accumulation of all of your life experience and generally knows the right course of action. We often second-guess or doubt this voice, or cannot access it because the clutter of the "monkey mind" and social conditioning and expectations of others. Doubts and chaos in our circumstances prevent us from the quiet contemplative state that allows intuition to arise. In my 2008 notes, I wrote: "intuition is body wisdom that comes from a combination of clarity of mind, heart wisdom, and fire in the belly." The shadow side, what happens when we don't trust our intuition, is control, ruthlessness, and a need to look good.

Invocation. This is giving voice to my intentions, and is similar to entreaty, affirmation, and prayer. All of them are ways to express our intentions. Invocation addresses the question, What can I bring forth? That makes invocation a future intention, whereas affirmations are typically in the present—what I want to create in myself right now.

What "I" words speak to you? What is your work at this time?

J is for Judgment

"The ability to observe without evaluating is the highest form of intelligence" --Jiddu Krishnamuri

My first year in the Four Fold Way™ yearlong, one evening I sat in the circle, projecting a calm exterior with neutral expression on my face and resisted my urge to fidget. I tried to watch with compassion and consider why almost everything about this woman annoyed me. The facilitator had just asked her a question about what she would do to change an unhealthy dynamic in her relationship. She screwed her face up, eyes closed tightly shut, lips pursed, head tilted to the heavens, and stuttered, stammered, and started over three times. Then she said she would rattle for ten minutes every morning. Inwardly I was rolling my eyes, but also relieved that at least she had not launched into one of the stories that I had heard at least four other times. I was wondering how rattling was going to change her relationship. My judgments triggered irritability, restlessness, and annoyance in the moment that interfered with my ability to stay present.

I was able to contain my judgments to my own head, but it wasn't until later that I could start to unpack them. I knew that my work was not to focus on why this particular person bothered me, but to look for the bigger triggers of judgment that applied in many areas of my life. But I could use the concrete behaviors of this specific person to help me identify those patterns.

Why did I judge the body posture that she often assumed when thinking? I realized that it felt inauthentic to me; it felt drama-laden and sometimes seemed a ploy to get attention. I remembered another person from my past who had demonstrated a similar body posture, and who had stirred up much drama in my life. Perhaps this current woman was a mirror of that person who had caused pain in my life.

I had noticed that she took up more air-time in group than anyone else. I recognized that I have judgments about what I labeled as "neediness." She was chronically late to group. I recognized that judgment came from my childhood experience, particularly from my father who insisted on being early everywhere we went. I absorbed a belief, taught by my parents and my community, that it was a hostile act to show up late. It was considered a sign of disrespect for the others in the group. I did not learn until later that other cultures had different views of time.

I had judgments about her long rambling stories. I found myself in unhealthy comparison when she talked, thinking about how I would NEVER behave in the ways she described. So I was considering myself superior to her. I judged her for being stuck in an old pattern. However, when I reflected on it, the only difference between us was that she told her old story out loud. I had learned to keep my old story to myself, but I was still stuck even if I did not foist my painful story on others anymore.

Finally, she often expressed the concern that she did not know who she was. As I reflected on this, I realized that I have little tolerance for people over the age of 50 who say this. I find it hard to believe that anyone could have so little self-awareness at this stage of life. Why did I have judgments about that? I spent so much of my free time in reflection about life and understanding myself. Yet here I am exploring why I'm so judgmental and I'm in my 60s. I don't know myself well enough to change this pattern, so who I am to judge?

When I tried to detach from the situation and view it from a more flexible perspective, I realized how painful it must be to be in her skin. She constantly fidgeted and had many physical health problems—almost every week she reported some new ailment. She could not sit quietly during meditations. She presented her life as very stressful. Could I focus on compassion when I listened to her the next time? What am I getting out of judgment; what is keeping me from changing? When I judge others, I get to feel superior. I get to shut down and time-travel and not really listen to the painful story and the even more painful secondary process. But when I shut down like that, my heart is closed. I do not express my judgments out loud, so other people still see me as a basically kind and compassionate person. It's my secret.

So how is it harming me? I can't really grow as a person if I hang on to my attachment to my judgments. I cannot develop into the kind of person I really want to be if I continue to judge others. I want to be a kind and compassionate person both inside and outwardly. The judgments obscure my wisdom voice. I could be learning so much more from others if I would really listen to them.

Angeles said that we all have two types of assumptions to get rid of: judging others and assuming that others are judging me. I have made a lot more progress in the second one. I still judge others regularly, but I am less inclined to even consider whether someone is judging me. Maybe that is part of my own judgmental nature to have a kind of narcissistic belief that I'm doing the judging and others are not judging me? In thinking about the concept of judgment, I did a lot of reading of wisdom texts and found this quote: "People hasten to judge in order not to be judged themselves" (Albert Camus). Maybe unconsciously that is what I'm doing. I have to track whether that might be true.

Another quote that rang true for me came from Earl Nightingale "When you judge others, you do not define them, you define yourself." That one stung a little, so I knew it was true. Every judgment I have is less about the other person than about my own character.

Our culture encourages us to put a value or judgment label on our experiences rather than just describe them objectively. A practice from meditation may help to soften judgments. This practice distinguishes between receptive vigilance: noticing what surfaces, and active vigilance, or putting a question or situation in front of myself for analysis during a meditation. The key is to describe without interpreting what it means; to observe with heightened curiosity.

I've been working on this for a long time, and I now name it when it happens, but so far, I don't always take an action to release my judgments. In past journal entries, I have actually written about forgiving myself for being so judgmental, but now it seems like a cop-out. I need to skill up and take more consistent actions to reduce this old pattern. The best advice I found so far, came from Reverend Jesse Jackson "Never look down on anybody unless you're helping them up."

How is the concept of judgment working you these days?

"J" Glossary

Jealousy. Jealousy stems from comparison and competition. If someone has a quality, a material good, a status, or a relationship that you strongly wish you had, and you compare yourself to that person, jealousy can result. Or maybe you think a person's love is a finite quality that you must compete with others to receive.

How much easier life would be if we did not compare and had gratitude for all the good in our lives, without coveting what others have. We can be happy for them, rather than jealous. Sometimes jealousy stems from insecurity: I feel that I am not good enough to keep that significant other happy, or my friendship is not enough to keep that person in my life, or that I am not interesting enough to be part of that group. The critical, self-doubting voices within create these situations, and if we express the jealousy, we are testing the relationship, putting it at risk.

Journaling. Angeles often noted the value of tracking your life and noted that journaling is one of the oldest tools for reflection and integration in the world. A journal can record what's working, the seeds of learning, track particular qualities that you need to pay attention to, and record gratitude. Re-reading journals and noting the insights that occur can provide the fodder for integration work.

Journey Work. Every season, Angeles would guide us in a different form of journey work; an extended period of meditation to shamanic drumming, click sticks, rattles, or music. The process was to imagine yourself in your spirit canoe with a male ancestor to your right, and a female ancestor to your left, and helper allies at your feet. Pay attention to everything you see and hear and experience on the journey. If you travel to the lower world, you will feel heavy, dense, exhausted, and are there for deep healing or soul retrieval work. If you travel to the upper world, you may feel light or even like you are flying or floating; you are there for guidance or expansion of spirit. If you stay in the middle world, you are focused on your own immediate body and need to take some action in your current outer world. If you do not remember or fall asleep, you were taken for healing work. It was important to journal about the experience afterwards and give the experience a title, so as to not forget any lessons you might have learned. Who appeared in your journey? What issues came up? Where did you go?

Joy. Angeles often encouraged us to track what brings us joy. We are often so focused on what is not working in life, that we miss the little expressions of joy and the beauty of the small things in life. Sometimes we lose track of the things that bring us joy, a resource of the heart and healing. One activity is to think about when we were age 8-12 years old. What did we do at that time for the sheer joy of it? What activities caused us to lose track of time? This activity might identify pieces of yourself to reclaim.

What "J" words speak to you? What is your work at this time?

K is for Kisses

At the end of a session, Angeles would announce "time for kisses." Angeles followed the physical gesture for throwing kisses with the words "you can't stay grumpy, mad, or sad when you throw kisses." Every session ended on this note, one of her most joyful quirky behaviors. The ritual demonstrated the value of staying positive, of leaving any encounter on a playful, fun note.

Angeles modeled so much in this simple practice; this ritual ending for sessions. It showed her gentle sense of humor, modeled one way to "end well," and it showed a positive regard for everyone in the room, fostering a sense of community.

This practice reminds me not to take myself too seriously, and not to elevate the content and teaching of knowledge or skills over relationship building and personhood development. It helps me stay connected to my funny bone. It also reminds me of the fact that Angeles conveyed several times over the years: that it takes three positive comments or behaviors to negate one negative comment. Making sure that one ends on a positive note may help to negate any negative aspects of the session. The practice of throwing kisses also brings a person into the present moment and is a way of showing gratitude to others in the group. It sends a message that even if we did some very deep inner work in the session, that we should revel in this work and find it joyful. It brought everyone in the group back to the present moment and out of the contemplative or reflective mode that characterized much of the group, and readied us to depart safely from the group. Throwing kisses is an embodied act; a physical expression of joy and connection. Finally, it is a closure ritual, sealing the session.

What joyful practices do you have to spread kindness to the world?

"K" Glossary

Kin. Kin, or family, came up in every session, as one of the biggest sources of transitions, such as births, deaths, weddings, anniversaries, reunions, and separations. Our first teachers of love and interpersonal communication are found in our family relationships. Angeles always said that relationship is a rigorous spiritual practice. Relationships between parents and children are different than other types of relationships and she often commented on the challenges of staying within the boundaries of parent/child and not trying to become a friend to a child. Nonattachment with children is one of the most challenging of all experiences. Angeles also noted that unconditional love is only possible in parent-child relationships and is not appropriate to other forms of relationship.

Kindness. In my 2013 journal, I noted the following saying, but did not write down the attribution:

> "If you can't be loving, be kind.
> If you can't be kind, be nonjudgmental.
> If you can't be nonjudgmental, then do no harm.
> If you can't do no harm, do the least harm possible."

Known and Unknown. These concepts are related to the comfort zone (the known and knowable) and the growing edge and breakthroughs; processes that take us into unknown territory. Angeles often said, "Trust in the mystery, but have a back up plan." That is, we can plan for possible futures without being attached to our plans. We should always prepare well, knowing that the mystery may set our plans aside.

What "K" words speak to you? What is your work at this time?

L is for Looping

"What we resist, persists" --Carl Jung

Looping is when a story gets stuck in the brain and repeats over and over without any resolution. Often, we embellish the story with every new telling, whether we are sharing the story with another or rehashing it in our minds. These loops are self-perpetuating, ensuring that we do not heal from the original trauma. Instead of healing, we get rewarded by the attention, sympathy, or negative bonding from others. Or we get energy from the attention we pay to the story in our own mind that inflates the issue into a big hairy deal. The actual facts of the original event may have been altered beyond recognition by this time, and the story has now been re-crafted to present our own part in the drama in a more favorable light, or as the "victim" of the villainous other.

I have one of those stories. The original events occurred many years ago. I felt "wronged" and treated unfairly because of the words and actions of another, let's call her X. X contributed to the loss of a relationship that was very important to me; someone I considered a "soul-mate." Let's call her Y. The behaviors of the "villain" in this story, X, were to tell lies about me. I was not leaping to assumptions, because she informed me directly that she was going to tell lies in order to destroy the relationship. But this was not the whole story. I did a few "less than becoming" things in my attempt to keep the relationship with Y, and I did not always take the high road—I leave these details out when I tell the story to others. When I am being brutally honest with myself, I can see how hanging on to the old story of being victimized only harms me, not the villainous X who does not even know that I continue to harbor resentment and anger toward her. It is so seductive to tell this version of the story—it has all the elements of an epic tragedy beginning with the rapturous love story with Y, then introducing the evil manipulator, X. It has true love thwarted by betrayal, major injustices committed, and insurmountable obstacles to being able to be together. By the end of the story, I qualify for sainthood and X for a life sentence in prison.

Each time I tell the story, I gradually build an even stronger case against the perpetrator. My listeners (the jury) are quick to denounce and pass judgment on this evil woman, and I get my revenge. Or do I? What have I gained by garnering the sympathy of my listener? It doesn't get my relationship back, nor does it allow me to forgive the manipulator X, who did what she did to protect her own relationship with the one I considered my soul-mate. I know her behaviors stemmed from jealousy and insecurity, but yet, I still loop on this old story that casts her as the unequivocal villain. I carry this grudge around like a heavy stone around my neck, keeping me from being a lighter, happier, and better human being. I use her as a scapegoat for everything that went awry in those chaotic few years.

Angeles often said that we loop on the same old sad stories for a couple of reasons. One might be that we do not feel heard. I have told the story to enough good friends who really listened, and I do feel heard, so that is not the motive for my hanging to the story. Another reason for looping, Angeles said, was that we did not want to change. The story was reaping some benefit, otherwise we would let it go. This feels true. I am getting something out of the story, a feeling of being special for having had this soul-mate experience with a truly extraordinary person that I would never have dreamed would love me back. To give up the story means that I have to see it realistically, and acknowledge that she played a role as well. She chose to believe the villain, not me. Maybe she was not really my soul-mate if she was capable of believing such lies. I put her on a pedestal, and if I am forced to see the reality of the story, the fairy-tale romance is tarnished. Who doesn't want a fairy tale romance in their lives? It makes me feel special. Now that I have identified the reason for hanging on to the story, my work is to figure out why I have yet to release it.

What stories loop in your mind? Why are you hanging on to them? What would your life be like without this old story?

"L" Glossary

Land. Angeles said that indigenous cultures believed that land shapes us in profound ways, and that we seek different type of land for different purposes. The woods/forests are best for deepening and integration work; mountains for gaining fresh perspectives; water for flexibility/fluidity work; and the desert for opening and balancing of the inner and outer worlds. Questions that help us to explore the significance of land include:

- What is the land that has shaped me the most?
- What is the land that I am most drawn to at this time?
- What is the land that I am least drawn to at this time?
- What is the most healing experience I've had in nature?
- What is the most challenging experience I've had in nature?
- What is my current relationship with nature?

Laws of Nature. The three laws of nature are: 1) everything in nature has a purpose; 2) everything is interdependent; and 3) everything is constantly changing and diversifying. The death/rebirth cycle is continually in motion.

Leadership. In my 2008 notes, I recorded Angeles' five qualities of leadership (warrior traits): courage, flexibility, patience, trust, and integrity. The shadow side of each, respectively, is paralysis/inaction, loss of sense of humor, arrogance/pride, control, and self-deception.

Legacy. A saying that Angeles often repeated was this African prayer:

> Let us take care of the children for they have a long way to go.
> Let us take care of the elders for they have come a long way.
> Let us take care of those in between, for they are doing the work.

Letting Go. Giving up attachments and old grudges is one of the hardest, but most critical things we can do in our quest for authenticity. Ultimately, we will do the biggest letting go: of our physical bodies. We have many opportunities to practice before we must face that final letting go. There is a great freedom associated with letting go. To let go, we have to figure out why we are still hanging on to an attachment; what are we getting out of it? If it only caused pain and we did not have some benefit from the attachment, we would have already changed and let go of it. The benefits of attachments can be related to fears, feeling special, getting attention, feeling "right" (or righteous), feeling in control, and many more.

Life. Angeles called life "the luminous pause between birth and death." Am I using the gift of life well? Am I doing what I came here to do? Angeles always said the two purposes of life are to love and to create.

Limits. See boundaries for discussion of limits and boundaries. In putting together this glossary, I had an insight about the difference between limits and boundaries and conditions. Angeles always said not to test relationships or put conditions on them, yet she also said we need clear limits and boundaries. I was always confused by this notion, thinking that a boundary and a condition were the same thing. It finally occurred to me that in logic, a conditional phrase is stated as an "if, then" statement. So in a relationship, a condition would be, "If you (lie to me, are untrue, etc), then I will (stop loving you, leave you, etc)." A limit and boundary is a clear statement of my needs. For example, "I will not tolerate infidelity in a relationship." The other person then knows the boundary and can behave accordingly. The condition is stated more like a threat than a clear limit and boundary.

Listening Practice. Really listening to a person and discerning both the content and feeling tone of their message is a critical skill to develop. Deep listeners use mountain countenance (no nodding, smiling, or commenting until the person is done talking) and listen to understand.

In this practice in small groups, each person practices listening deeply as the first person presents a current situation that is challenging them. Then the listeners consider "What questions would help move the person to resolution?" Sometimes the questions are framed as "Have you considered..." This framing presents different alternatives that the speaker may not have considered. Others might also ask, "What matters most to you about this being resolved?" This question gets at whether the resolution comes from the heart or the ego. After each person has had a turn to speak and to be a listener/questioner, in the final round, each person shares the impact of the other group members questions. What did I learn from the other person's experience and the way that they framed questions to me?

Other things to consider about myself as a listener: Do I rehearse what I'm going to say while the other person is still talking? Do I check out? Do I have judgments?

In my 2011 journal from a mentoring workshop, Angeles said "Pay attention to what people say with their hand on the door as they are leaving." These words often convey the things of the heart that are hard to say. Another time she said to pay attention to what a person leads with. They often lead with the heart issue, but unconsciously it frightens them, so they deviate from it in what follows. So the hard things are often presented at the beginning or end of a conversation.

Love. Love is the resource of the healer and has several arms: acknowledgment, gratitude, generosity, and joy. If we test our love, it takes us out of love. If we are always talking about our relationship to others, chances are we are not present in the relationship. If we are playing for attention and have need for reassurance, we are tentative, distrustful, or not fully engaged in our relationships. Over-processing kills relationships. A healthy relationship is characterized by:

      1) clear requests;
      2) recognition that it is always changing;
      3) the fact that all problems are co-created and shared—
we each contribute to any challenge.

We need to know what we can truly accept in another, and what are our "non-negotiables" (behaviors or traits in another that are incompatible with our core values or cross our boundaries and limits). If we do commit to a relationship, the conscious withholding of love is mean-spirited.

Angeles said that divorces and separations are most common in the spring, when we are fully present to the resource of love and less likely to settle for less than we deserve. Some tracking questions about love are:

- What pattern in my relationship do I want to change?
- What obstacles do I let get in the way of loving?
- Where do I withhold or withdraw love?
- Who are my teachers of love at this time?

In 2011, Angeles said that four domains of love are found in many different cross-cultural contexts, such as the Four Immeasurables of Buddhism, and the Four Treasures in Hindu writing. These four include:

1. Compassion
2. Empathic joy
3. Loving kindness (comes from self-trust)
4. Equanimity

Every relationship consists of three lines: my line, your line, and the relationship line. The goals of each line are not always in alignment. Sometimes one partner is in an individuation phase that causes some separation, and people in relationships grow at different rates. It is important to pay attention to all three lines.

Luck. This is the space "where opportunity and preparedness intersect." As Angeles always said, "Trust in the mystery but have a back-up plan." That is, we should plan and prepare well, but know that our plans may have to be abandoned.

Lying Meditation. This is a tool of the healer. See Journey Work. Angeles modeled lying meditation using silence, music, drumming, rattles, and click sticks. Each modality triggers a different type of experience.

What "L" words speak to you? What is your work at this time?

M is for Manifestation

"The word is a force you cannot see, but you can see the manifestation of that force, the expression of the word, which is your own life." --Don Miguel Ruiz

The first one-on-one conversation I had with Angeles, at my first weeklong foundation training, she said, "You are a manifester." I didn't really know what she meant at the time, and wondered how she could know much of anything about me with such limited exposure. I had been sitting in the circle for three days, but had not spoken up in the large group at all.

Later, I realized that manifestation was one of my unacknowledged gifts and talents. When I put my mind to something, I generally follow-through and make it happen. What a gift it was to have Angeles point it out to me, so that I could own it and consciously access this gift more consistently when I needed it. As I have studied it more carefully, I am starting to see what qualities or characteristics make up manifestation. The word comes from the Latin root "caught in the act" and "flagrant." So it means to make something visible; to create something that can be detected by the senses from the original invisible ideas. Manifestation takes vision, patience, persistence, and action.

Manifestation requires first developing a vision, and then keeping that vision before you throughout the rest of the process. It is easy to get distracted by small details that lead to going down a different path and losing track of the bigger vision.

Some tasks are short-term projects with clear evidence of manifestation—you finish that report for work and there it is, neatly stapled on your boss's desk. Other things, like life dreams, require a long process of manifestation, and may appear in phases. They may take several trial and error episodes before manifesting in the way you imagined. You may manifest a new job or a new relationship or a new talent.

I have learned that, for me, the vision comes fairly easily, but sometimes I stall because of lack of patience and persistence, or I let the idea stay in my head and don't take action. I have learned the things that get me stuck: if the process has what I label as tedious tasks, like detailed numbers, calculations, or picky formatting. If I have to learn or install a new software program, and it does not go smoothly, I may abandon the task at least for a while. If I have to learn something totally new to me, and the number of resources (energy, need to take lessons, do a lot of reading) to learn it is too great, I can get overwhelmed. I hardly ever get stalled if there is an intellectual challenge to solve—that is what excites and motivates me to persist. I have been able to manifest well in terms of creating my new life and in terms of writing. These are both facets of my life dream and sometimes I am surprised how things fall into place once I am clear about my vision.

But manifestation goes well beyond just "finish what you start." It's not merely task completion. What sets it apart is the vision part of it. Angeles always said, "If I can see it and name it, I can manifest it." The step between naming it and manifesting it requires one or more of the fires of vision: the creative fire, the passion that is our love nature, the fire of transformative change. It's harder to manifest out of duty or obligation, although many of us manage to do it if required by our jobs or relationships. This type of manifestation does not bring joy and fulfillment.

Angeles proposed four phases of manifestation (Triumphs of the Imagination workshop with Angeles and Patrick O'Neill, 2005):

1. Inspiration: the phase of generating ideas, and the incubation of vision;
2. Discovery, exploration, and evaluation: the phase of trying out the ideas and seeing how they work;
3. Re-formulation and testing: the phase of working out the bugs, and getting it right. This stage might involve a period of re-thinking: What have I not thought of yet? There is a need to be proactive rather than reactive. Reactivity is a response that waits for other people or the environment to initiate an action; proactivity is self-initiating;
4. Implementation and celebration.

Manifesting life dreams involves leaving our comfort zone and challenging our assumptions. It involves looking at our own defensiveness and reactivity, and giving those up. We have to stay open to the process. It requires a willingness to be coached or accept help, a willingness to be accountable and a commitment to be responsible. It requires full engagement and a balance between taking initiative and seeking help from others. Finally, it takes a combination of patience and persistence. These goes hand in hand, because the process may be long and sometimes challenging. But the end product is well-worth the effort as we find ourselves living in our own life dream.

What is your relationship to manifestation? Is there something in your life that you need to manifest now? How can you go about it? What is the first step?

"M" Glossary

Magnetism. This is what energy we draw to us. When we are open, authentic, and focusing on our gifts and talents, we attract the positive in our lives. When we are negative or needy, we pull that kind of energy to us. Angeles often told the story from the Native American tradition that we all have two wolves within us, one of good and the other of evil. When asked which one will win, the answer is "the one we feed." We can consciously feed the good. Magnetism is one of the life forces along with dynamism and integration. A human's magnetic field extends about 12 feet around us, and shows our emotions and attitudes. An observant person can see it, and even non-observant people sometimes pick up on our "energy." We can control how we present to others to some extent. When I am not tending to my magnetism, I can become pre-occupied, distant, and closed off to others. Alternatively, I may be projecting all kinds of anxiety and negative energy.

Manufactured Fear. Angeles noted that only rarely are our fears grounded in reality (primal fears); most of the time, they are manufactured in the mind by our thoughts and past stories of trauma. Sometimes we manufacture traumas because of a high need for attention; we lapse into using drama, victimization, and catastrophizing to bond with others. This is an example of emotional indulgence and is the place of the child, not the mature adult. Fear constricts our energy and creativity. Asking questions about the feelings can shift the energy and reduce the fear. What am I afraid will happen? Is it based in reality? If I can name the fear, I can change it.

Mastery. The road to mastery in any new endeavor is "do it wrong until I get it right." We need to have compassion for self and others and allow mistakes. Learning occurs when we integrate our mistakes into past experiences.

Mature Love. This is in contrast to infatuation, the false sense of love that comes from romantic and sexual attractions. Mature love involves deepening of intimacy, and growth for the individuals and the relationship line. If we do not have mature love, we look for the fire outside of the relationship. We can ask ourselves: How have I fostered intimacy in my relationships?

Have I allowed my significant others to be themselves? Do I test my relationship? Angeles labeled testing of relationships as an act of arrogance. To withhold love is the definition of mean-spirited. Have I closed my heart and become cynical about love? Have I put conditions on my love? To do so opens the doorway to dis-ease. An open heart is discerning—it puts limits and boundaries on my relationships, but not conditions. Every relationship needs space and time for each individual, balanced with quality time together. In every relationship, there is my life dream/purpose, the other person's life dream/purpose, and the relationship line to attend to.

Medicine Bags. These are objects that one creates and then keeps by the bedside to help with healing or manifestation. Once the healing happens or the manifestation comes true, burn it or bury it. To create the medicine bag, write a sacred intention on a piece of white paper. Wrap it along with some kernels of corn in a green piece of cloth and tie it with string. The white paper symbolizes the idea that every day is a blank canvas. We get to start anew each day to manifest our intentions and goals. The corn represents all our gifts and talents. Which ones am I using? Which am I not using, and need to befriend? Count them and name them. The green cloth represents what I want to regenerate or renew in my life. Finally, the string symbolizes my life journey. Am I fully engaged in my own life? What is getting in the way of living my own authentic life? Take at least one action every day to support the breakthrough I want.

Mentoring (as opposed to teaching, coaching, advising). A mentor is a person who carries wisdom and is flexible, warm, and solid/grounded. They serve in their full sufficiency and never give unsolicited advice. Angeles elevated mentoring to a higher-level type of guidance to others than:

- teaching is conveying/sharing information or skills,
- coaching is helping the person with the goals they set themselves to address current problems,
- counseling is deep healing work focused on the past, and
- advising is specific to a particular need, such as professional counseling about careers.

A mentor shows the person things that they do not see themselves. We can only take others as far as our own work has taken us. To be a good mentor, we must keep growing ourselves. Mentors ask questions that are disorienting, or on unfamiliar ground, but do not give unsolicited advice. A mentor may send the person away to do healing work first. The primary goal of mentoring is to move people into their own sufficiency and help them grow. A good mentor has ample patience and humility, and will disturb the mentee. Disturbance in Angeles' context, means stepping out of one's comfort zone and growing. In a 2010 mentoring workshop, Angeles noted three portals of growth that mentors can help mentees explore:

1. work I have done already (builds sufficiency, confidence)
2. work I haven't done yet (outlines the next steps)
3. work I need to do now

Some questions that might help identify those portals include:

- Is the life you're living your own life? If not, why?
- What truths do you need to face and act upon?
- What or who do you allow to trigger your insecurities?
- What will you do with the good years you have left?
- What consistent positive feedback have you received this year?
- What challenging feedback have you received this year?

Mirrors. Angeles used mirrors in a variety of ways to encourage people to go deeper. Almost universally, a moan would rise up from the circle when the mirrors appeared—we all knew that mirror work was hard. A mirror is a projection of part of myself that's on its way home, otherwise I wouldn't be able to see it. Here are a few examples of mirror work from my notes.

Mirror Activity #1.
This activity is done in groups of 3-4 people so that each person can be witnessed and witness others. In three rounds of questions, each person looks into the mirror and talks to his/her self, using these prompts:

When I look in the mirror, I see...
What I want you to see about me is...
What I don't want you to see is....

Angeles noted that where we want to be seen are our gifts and talents; what we don't want seen are our insufficiencies, doubts, and vulnerabilities. But when we try to hide them, we are not whole. They are areas that are underdeveloped or places where we lack courage.

Mirror Activity #2.
Another activity with mirrors posed these questions:

> Here is what I do to look good...
> What triggers my need to look good?
> Here is why I feel I need to look good...
> Underneath my need to look good is...
> If I didn't have to look good, I would...

Mirror Activity #3.
In the next activity, done in the whole circle, we consider whether other members of the group are serving as mirrors to our own experiences. There are a number of different types of mirrors:

- **Clear mirror**: this person teaches us about our best self. If I see it in another person, I have it in me as well. I can own it. A clear mirror is a person who captures our imagination and who carries a lot of positive energy for us—someone who ignites the fires of inspiration.
- **Neutral mirror**: this is a person I'm so comfortable with that I can just be myself. I need no effort or performance and feel calm and at home with this person.
- **Smoking mirror**: This person shows where my shadow work is; I'm projecting my own stuff on another person. The person who irritates and annoys me can be my best teacher related to shadow work. This person may spark competition, jealousy, or envy (comparison). They bring up "unfinished business" or remind us of someone from our past.
- **Split mirror:** There are two types. In the fire type of split mirror, this is a person that I might be sexually attracted to. It's important to acknowledge these attractions to avoid feeding off the sexual energy and sending a mixed message. In the power-type of split mirror, this is the person to whom I give away my power. It's someone that I may have approval needs with, or don't totally trust.

- **No mirror:** This is the person that I have not seen or interacted with. It is important to discern why this person has not registered with me—why have I overlooked this unique individual? This person may represent a part of myself that I have subconsciously rendered invisible.

In the activity, the mirrors are in the center of the circle. As each mirror is described, a member of the circle can take a mirror from the center and place it front of another person and explain what impact that person has had on them; what type of mirror they are.

Mountain Countenance. This is the embodiment of presence and deep listening, when we do not nod, smile, or show much emotion. It is the face of concentration and attention, of benign regard. It does not detract from the message of the other.

Movements (of every day). In my 2012 journal, Angeles did an activity that involved tracking the "three great movements" of each day:

1. Receiving. What was revealed to me or given to me today? Was I open to receiving?
2. Offering. What invitations, opportunities, or possibilities showed up today? Did I meet these with curiosity? Where did I offer invitations, opportunities, or possibilities to others?
3. Choosing/Selecting. What choices did I make today?

These three create repeating cycles: If I am open to receiving, I am aware of the offerings of the day and can make wise choices.

The Mystery's Plan. Another favorite saying of Angeles' was: "There's my plan and there's the mystery's plan." This indicated the need to be flexible and not attached to outcome, since the mystery often works us and disrupts our attempts to control our circumstances.

What "M" words speak to you? What is your work at this time?

N is for Nonattachment

Nonattachment, according to Angeles, is the capacity to care deeply from a place of openness to outcome and deep engagement. As a psychologist, I had been educated in attachment theory, the idea that a healthy affectional bond between parent and child is the foundation for healthy relationships in adulthood. If you as a child could not rely on your parents, it set the stage for problems with all relationships to come. Attachment is a feeling that binds one to a person, cause, ideal, or things. It means to join and connect with another. I was raised to think of attachment as a positive human quality. Learning to let go of attachments and be more objective is one of the hardest of the lessons I have learned from Angeles, and one that I have struggled with mightily. I have to constantly remind myself that nonattachment is not the same thing as detachment, which implies a disengagement and not caring. The problem is not feeling a bond with people or things, but having expectations for how those bonds should be manifest or how things should turn out. It's attachment to *outcomes* that is the problem.

Angeles' philosophy, along with that of many other traditions, teaches that attachments to outcomes can create an unhealthy rigidity. When we are attached, we lose perspective, become fixed in one viewpoint, get too serious, and cannot see the alternatives. One area where I am still firmly attached is to my work identity. When I'm attached to an identity, I automatically want others to see me in a particular way that is consistent with that identity. Therefore, I am tempted to put on a mask or create a false-self that is consistent with that identity. I lose the ability to see other ways of being that honor my work profession but do not have me firmly attached to being a certain kind of professor.

Nonattachment requires strong gifts of wisdom, equanimity, respect, and compassion. It also takes courage to let go of that which no longer serves us—old stories and old patterns of behaviors from the past. We have to take into account what it has cost us to hold on to this attachment.

One other way that attachment has been hurting me in recent years, especially since the year of my mother's death and dying process, is how over-identification with my current identities, roles, and memories has been keeping me from reaching some sense of peace around my own death. I do not have a strong faith practice that reassures me about death. I do not believe in a heaven or hell. Other traditions, like reincarnation, or a void, also offer me no comfort. What is the use in having another life after this one if I don't have any memory of this life? The idea of emptiness or nothingness is also a terrifying thought because I'm so attached to my current life. I'm extremely challenged in thinking of myself without those identities and roles and memories. This attachment leaves me unable to consider any alternatives that leave behind my identities and roles and allow the possibility of some level of transcendence. As I move through the decade of my 60s, it feels more pressing to address these questions and consider who I am beyond my identities and roles. In a few years, I hope to retire. How will I define myself without my work identity? It has been such a major part of my life, but it is not me. The next challenge will be defining myself beyond "me." How can I separate from my attachment to a life as me, a unique being? Will I be able to accept my connection to a larger world where those identities do not matter? Stay tuned...there is a serious inside job ahead.

Where do you have attachments to outcomes at this time in your life? How are you working to release those attachments?

"N" Glossary

Naming: "If you can name it, you can change it," Angeles said. She asked us to title our experiences and name our fears, doubts, emotions, thoughts, and challenges. We also need to name our insights and accomplishments—the good things as well as the obstacles and challenges. Getting them out in the open and naming them allows us to access them more directly. Then we can see our underlying motives, old patterns of responding, and/or expectations, so that we can change them. One particularly useful form of naming is to notice when I'm telling myself a story. When I accurately name it as "story," I remind myself that I created this story in my mind and it may not be true or current. When I name a feeling, I remind myself that I should not make decisions or act when in a reactive, emotional state. Naming the feeling may help me to let go of it, rather than indulge it. When I name a seed of learning from the day, I increase the chances that I will integrate it into my personhood and grow.

Nature. The word "nature" has many meanings: at minimum it refers to our internal "natural" way of being (authentic self) and the outer world (Mother Nature) that supports our survival. Angeles promoted bridging of the two, so that we have greater appreciation and support for our external world to preserve and save it for future generations. She also promoted a state of being natural and expressing our true selves. To get at our true nature, she might ask, "Who are you beyond your roles and identities?" This is one of the major transitions of the second half of life: to better integrate the inner and outer worlds.

Nature's Rhythm. Is medium to slow. Angeles often talked about the harm of our too-fast, driven culture, and encouraged us to slow down to nature's rhythm as often as possible to get in touch with our own natures. The wisdom voice is buried when we are too busy and moving at breakneck speed. It needs quiet, calm, and slowing down to emerge. In addition, healing work must take place at nature's rhythm.

Negative Bonding. This is when a friendship or relationship is based on "dumping one's garbage on each other." Angeles said that in indigenous cultures, one would never share their negative stories and insufficiencies with family and friends, but instead take these issues to a wise person, elder, sage, or healer. This type of venting to another person is an abuse of friendship and toxic to both; it is an act of arrogance. Instead, we can give our loved ones the "highlights" or report on our progress with difficult issues, but leave out the stories and the drama. Another alternative practice is to tell our stories to trees or boulders and ask for healing. There is power in giving voice to our experience and saying it out-loud (see "naming"). However, our friends cannot help us, because our answers are within and as adults, it's our responsibility to deal with our own emotional baggage. There is no reason that friends and loved ones should have to suffer along with us. Angeles suggested that if we have others in our lives who vent to us, we should listen the first time, then the second time ask "What have you done about this since the last time we talked?" If the friend brings up the same issue a third time, ask them to take the issue to counseling or other professional or spiritual help. A true friendship is an intimate heart connection, in the present, not the past.

"Neurosis is the narrowing of the spiritual landscape" (Carl Jung)

No is a complete sentence. Angeles noted that we do not have to give excuses or rationalize a "no." No does not mean I don't like you. Similarly, saying yes, does not mean that we agree with the person's ideas, only that we are acknowledging a course of action or idea. If we say no more often, we make the "yes" more meaningful. We can say no to things that violate our limits and boundaries or take us out of the authentic self.

Noble Silence. Stay in silence if the time or place is not right, or if you cannot speak without blame or judgment. Noble silence may avoid escalating conflict and is needed in times of reactivity—do not speak if you are in doubt or too emotional.

What "N" words speak to you? What is your work at this time?

O is for Openness

"The door is round and open....do not go back to sleep" --Rumi

When I first started seriously thinking of moving across the country, I found myself drawn to photos or paintings of doors. I was excited about the prospect of entering the door to a brand new life, not knowing what was on the other side of the door. The open door or window is a good symbol for this concept of openness. It has so many applications in Angeles' work: being open hearted, open to outcome, open-minded and flexible, open to opportunities, and open for business! Openness implies optimism. It is cheery and feels very present. The opposite is to be closed off and shut down.

I have reflected a lot on where I am not open, and what circumstances trigger me to shut down. Some of those are:

- When my judgmental nature gets triggered and I jump to a conclusion and develop a fixed assumption.
- When fear constricts me and causes me to close off in defense.
- When I am afraid of how others will perceive me; I am often not open to activities that might make me "look foolish." This fear of looking foolish is a strange one and I wonder where it comes from. I can clearly see from an evolutionary standpoint that some fears stem from the potential for actual harm, but how did we as humans come to consider being embarrassed as a form of harm?

I have learned that there is a relationship between my physical posture and my inner sense of openness. Angeles talked about crossed arms as a signal of being closed, although sometimes people cross their arms when cold or when they have back pain. I have chronic back pain, and often cross my arms when I have to stand or sit in one position for too long. I believe that this physical trait has encouraged close-heartedness and skepticism at times. Now I am more aware of when and why I cross my arms, and try to spend more time in an open position physically, so that I can be more open and receptive in every way. An open body increases our capacity to take in more information in a more curious fashion. Standing meditation also helps to increase openness, and

110

builds self-esteem and self-respect. Standing for 30 minutes a day shifts power and increases our capacity to be seen. It alters the energy field around us, our atmosphere.

One challenge in the past several years that triggers me to shut down is dealing with the physical changes associated with aging. I am good, even thrilled, about the changes in my life perspectives and growing wisdom, and my changes in lifestyle to allow for more time in nature for reflection work, but the physical changes are harder to accept. At times, I am terrified by the implications, as I move closer and closer to the ultimate letting go. I have no faith perspective to help me feel ease around dying, and instead of embracing this inevitable part of the cycle of humankind and all living beings, I shut down, distract myself, and deny. This may be one of the major lessons for me in this decade, or I will continue to suffer. Being closed off and rigid means to be breakable. When I am truly open, I can request each day, "Let me be guided to learn what I need to learn today" rather than trying to control or manipulate. As Angeles said, even if my physical body has limitations, I still have endless possibilities for growth and creativity.

Angeles always asked us to track our progress at the end of a season. Where did I open? This was along with tracking deepening, softening, and strengthening? Where did I become more receptive to different ideas or trying out new behaviors? Where did I open to acknowledging my sufficiency and owning my gifts and talents?

What helps you stay open, even in the face of fears? What work do you have to do related to opening yourself?

"O" Glossary

Observation. Observations are facts, devoid of judgments. When we observe patterns in other people, they are discernments rather than evaluations. For example, we might learn that this person in our life is not trustworthy when they are stressed, so we should not rely on them. We can discern that a particular relationship is not meeting our needs or is causing harm to us, and decide to leave, based on observation of the facts. Tracking tools are good ways to observe. The "fair witness" uses observations to gather information for decision-making.

Optimism. If we are positive and focus on what works, we feed the positive energy and draw more of it to ourselves. Angeles' focus on sufficiency, gratitude, and generative speaking also speak to maintaining a more positive outlook on life as necessary for personal growth.

Order. Angeles noted that clutter, or unnecessary stuff in the material or inner, spiritual world, upsets the simple beauty of the world, and is an obstacle to healing work. She often recommended an Asian practice for the material clutter; "move, give away, or throw out 27 items a day for 9 days and your life will change." Nine is the number of completion (27 = 2 + 7 = 9).

Original Medicine. Angeles always said that we are each unique beings with our own special gifts and talents and personhood, nowhere duplicated anywhere else in the world. We have distinctive voices, fingerprints, and retinal patterns, and respond to the world in the way that is a combination of our past experiences and our natural character. When in a group or relationship, we can draw from each person's original medicine to help us in our own journey of growth and healing.

Operating System. The process of putting together this book led me to lots of reflections on how and why this program works so well for so many. It turns out I have been thinking about this for a long time. The story that integrated my seeds of learning after the 2011 vision quest was about the "operating system" of the Four Fold Way™. Here is that story:

Four Fold Way ™ Technical Manual:
User's Guide To Getting Started

The Four Fold Way ™, Version 4.0, is a cross-cultural educational program designed to optimize individual personal growth and enhance relationships with self, others, community and nature. This user's guide provides step-by-step instruction on getting started with the program.

Included in the box:
- One brilliant teacher
- One detailed manual (The FFW book)
- 20-30 important strangers
- Hundreds of tracking tools and sage sayings
- CD software for application to daily life including 4 archetype modules to guide your progress to breakthrough

You will need to provide:
- Humility
- An open heart
- Commitment to change
- A power source: preferably connect to intention and consistent daily action for right use of power
- Gifts and talents not included: please supply your own

Operating System: STM 6.2
The Slow-to-Medium (STM) Operating System has been refined over years of use to produce exactly the right speed of processing to lead to breakthrough. Do not tamper with the processing speed of the program as increased speed is potentially harmful to the integrity of the modules.

Getting Started: Assembly
Connect the funny bone to the backbone to create a strong foundation, and then attach the deep, deep roots to the grounding wire. Download the archetype modules and attach to your long tall body. Add the warrior module to the north, followed by the healer component to the south, and the visionary module to the east, and then, when all the other pieces are firmly established, add the teacher component in the west. Finally, call on the ancestors and the helper allies, and now you are ready to use the FFW in everyday life.

Basic Operations: Using the FFW Program

The program is best used in the safety of a group with guidance from a wise teacher. Best results are obtained when starting with the warrior module to develop the presence and courage needed to tackle the other components of the program. Be mindful of staying in the formidable middle, as deviation to either extreme uses too much memory and adversely affects program effectiveness. Switch on your own gifts and talents to personalize the system to your own specifications. Each new module will activate at the appropriate season. Tracking tools are available in pop-up menus and are highly recommended for recording progress.

Advanced Modules

The CD also contains higher-level modules for tooling up in communication, patience, trust, integrity, authenticity, conflict resolution, compassion, and flexibility. Be sure to stretch thoroughly before initiating the flexibility module to avoid injury. If critical voices manifest, access the Curiosity Tool and the Shape-Shifting Wizard to override the negative programming of the doubting critical voices. Prolonged exposure of the system to judgmental voices can make the program susceptible to the self-doubt virus and looping worms.

Trouble-Shooting Tips

If the program does not seem to be working, follow these four tips to check the functionality of the modules.

1. Are you showing up and being present to the program? If not, check whether you engaged the on switch.
2. Are you telling yourself the truth about your own behavior without blame or judgment? If not, engage the Wisdom Generator.
3. Are you doing what has heart and meaning for you? If not, insert the healer module and re-boot your system.
4. Are you open, not attached to outcome? If not, check the settings in your own life to ensure that you are being alerted to positive results not expected or anticipated by your usual programming.

If you have addressed all of these questions, and are still not achieving breakthrough, check your seeds of learning in the cookies file and initiate the integration function. As a last resort, consider running a full diagnostic program to identify system malfunctions. The Vision Quest module offers one type of diagnostic analysis.

For 24-Hour Technical Support

Extensive and gentle technical support is readily available to users. Access www.angelesarrien.com or consult the detailed user manual, The Four Fold Way™.

What "O" words speak to you? What is your work at this time?

P is for Presence

"We convince by our presence" Walt Whitman

A few years ago, I conducted a small research study of a group of *Four Fold Way*™ participants in an attempt to discover why the program was so useful to people, and why many returned to Angeles' circle year after year. I developed a short survey of the characteristics of each archetype, measured shadow qualities, asked people what changes they had made, and why they thought this program worked for them. Although I learned a few interesting facts, the major finding was that people kept coming back because of Angeles' presence. It was her personhood that mattered most, rather than the specifics of what she taught. Many noted that they had other teachers in their lives, but none approached the level of integrity and wisdom of Angeles. Over and over, participants described her as their role model for living an authentic life. When she entered a room, everyone took notice. She commanded attention, not by being a celebrity, guru, or by having power over others, but through her humility and absolute self-sufficiency. She embodied all four archetypes as a complete package. I once read that presence is the opposite of powerlessness. Angeles did not seem "powerful" in the way that we usually use this word in our culture, but she certainly had presence. She was a very powerful force in the world in the spiritual sense.

So, I often wonder how I can better channel Angeles and be that wise presence to people in my life. Can I walk that path, aligning my life dream and my values with my behavior? I have all the tools, because Angeles freely revealed all the "secrets" of her own success as a teacher and mentor and outlined the path. But do I have the courage and discipline to live up to her model? Those tiny shoes are extraordinarily hard to fill. And I know that she was original medicine, and that I will embody presence in my own way.

Some of the characteristics that are inherent in a person with great presence are deep listening, a strong vision, integrity, curiosity, and sufficiency. In terms of deep listening, I still struggle to stay present in a conversation without being triggered to time-travel by something the other said, or to focus on formulating my response, thus missing important cues in the rest of the conversation. I lament my lack of "presence of mind" in these situations and often have the right question or comment only hours later. It turns out, I'm not alone in this.

There is a story of French philosopher Denis Diderot, who was invited to a dinner party with other intellectuals of the day. At one point, he was challenged on some point he was making, and to his chagrin, found himself at a complete loss for words. Humiliated by this experience, he found an excuse to leave soon after, and as he mulled over the conversation in his head on the way down the stairs, the perfect answer came to him. Of course it was too late. He coined the term "l'esprit d'escalier" or "staircase wit" to describe this phenomenon. This inability to stay present and think on our feet diminishes our projection of presence.

Angeles said that most people are not present to a conversation for more than five minutes before checking out. I know this is true for me. I'd like to work on this, and extend the respect that others deserve to be fully seen and heard. As I think about how Angeles structured small group work, she usually gave each person three minutes to speak; on rare occasions up to five minutes per person, but never more than that. I wonder if it was deliberate to avoid the tendency of members to check out during longer monologues. That's a lesson I can use in my own teaching: keep the time frame short to maintain the listener's attention (and to keep the speaker from going into long story).

Another quality of the person with presence is vision. Angeles said, "If I can see it in another person, then I have it in me, otherwise I wouldn't be able to see it." Can I see beyond the words and actions of the other person to the bigger picture? What am I projecting or mirroring in the other? What is their stuff, and what is my own in this conversation or interaction? Can I really see another person as a unique individual without making assumptions or having expectations? Angeles had a clear vision of herself as a teacher—there was never any doubt to anyone who witnessed her.

Angeles modeled standing in her integrity and being authentic. It was palpable. She lived her life according to the principles of the *Four Fold Way*™ and taught by example as well as directly teaching us skills.

Amy Cuddy, in a book called *Presence: Bringing Your Boldest Self to Your Biggest Challenges* said: "The ideal effect of presence [is that] you execute with comfortable confidence and synchrony, and you leave with a sense of satisfaction and accomplishment, regardless of the measurable outcome." This reminded me of Angeles' concept of sufficiency. When you lead with your sufficiency, you are seen as a person with power.

In terms of sufficiency, Angeles never expressed self-doubt, confusion, or lack of self-esteem. She did not exhibit arrogance, unhealthy pride, or irritations. She stayed firmly on the middle path in equanimity. That presence was reassuring, built safety, and created trust. When I am full of self-doubts and model insufficiency, my power is diminished and my presence is not comforting or reassuring to others. I may elicit sympathy, pity, or concern, but I don't have presence. When I can trust in myself, even if I don't know exactly how I will handle some situation, I can be sure that I have whatever resource is needed. I know that I will, in fact, be able to handle whatever is at my gate. I don't have to have all the answers ahead of time to be fully present. I can track whether I am showing up and being present in my life. I can note what triggers me to go AWOL...the things I judge as boring, annoying, beneath me, or too painful to witness.

What an honor and privilege it was to be in the presence of one who so embodied presence.

What feedback do you receive about your quality of presence? How can you cultivate this aspect of your personhood?

"P" Glossary

Pandora's Box. In my 2013 journal, I recorded Angeles' re-telling of the story of Pandora's Box. She said that there are cross-cultural variations on the story. All of them have one thing in common: when Pandora opened the box, all the evils entered the world. But there are different accounts of what was left in the bottom of the box. The common thread is that they are all overlooked parts of ourselves. In Asian cultures, what was left was compassion; in western stories, it was hope; and in Pacific Island cultures, truth. Angeles said these three qualities are the golden keys of relationships.

Parents. Angeles said that the loss of a father puts a person on a journey to achieve their dreams, and the loss of a mother starts one on a soul's journey. It takes at least a year for grieving to lessen.

Patience. So much of our personal growth hinges on patience, the ability to stay present through times of uncertainty or mundane or disliked tasks without showing or feeling irritation or annoyance. Humor and curiosity help us to stay in patience. When we feel impatient, it is often related to triggering the inner critic or expectations of how things should be. Patience requires empathy and therefore, leads to greater compassion, generosity of spirit, and kindness. The shadow sides of patience are arrogance, fear, and control. When we are impatient, we put the situation over the person, making the event more important than the relationship. Patience needs to be tracked in regards to how we view ourselves as well as how we interact with others. There is no such thing as "waiting patiently;" according to Angeles, we are either patient or we are waiting.

Personhood. Angeles referred to our authentic nature, character, and gifts and talents as representing our personhood, and said it was more important than the products of our labor, our identities, or roles. Who am I outside of those roles and identities? That is my personhood. It is who I am when I am being rather than doing. Personhood is opposed to ego, which contains the roles, identities, and expectations of others.

Portals. These are gateways, openings to some new learning. Portals to personal growth can include meditation, silence, prayer, time spent in nature, and many others. The gate or portal signals the boundary of your comfort zone.

Positionality. When you become attached to a certain outcome, you may formulate a strong position in favor of that outcome that makes you rigid and unable to see any alternatives. Positionality is a fixed and narrow perspective.

Potential. In one of Angeles' humorous stories, she related taking a class of some sort, where the teacher said she had "potential." She interpreted this comment as meaning that she was "crummy now." She urged us not to think of potential as a place of success, but as an indicator that we need to keep working to change.

Power (right use of). Power is the major resource of the warrior, or leader, who must learn to use power wisely and to the benefit of the most people. Power comes from a unique alignment of gifts and talents, tests of challenge, character qualities (humor, compassion, honesty, flexibility, etc) and skills (like communication, negotiation, people skills, bridge-building). Whenever I find myself judging, comparing, competing, jealous, or in envy, I am not using power wisely, and have self-esteem or compassion work to do. When I am in my full sufficiency, I use power wisely. I do not give away my power to appease or get approval.

Prayer. The practice of prayer is present in all religions and all cultures in various forms. Angeles said there are three kinds of prayers:

- Devotional: praying for the wellbeing of others.
- Petitionary: asking for help for oneself. For example, the practice of asking each day, "What resource would help me today?"
- Worship: giving thanks or honoring gods, nature, or the mystery.

Prayer Arrow Ceremony. When you need a breakthrough in your life, a sacred ritual may help. This ritual can be found in Central America and Africa. You ask/pray for guidance on how to achieve this breakthrough as you create the prayer arrow. Use a stick of 12-18 inches and wrap it in yarn in silence, contemplating the breakthrough you want to occur. The colors of yarn used in the ceremony have meaning and you can select some of all of the colors, or just the ones that most speak to you:

- Blue = clarity (Sky)
- Green = creativity and healing (Earth)
- Red = fire, the spiritual road (Fire)
- Black = surrender, trust, letting go (The Mystery)
- Yellow = dynamic energy and manifesting (Sun)
- White = the light into darkness; being open to experience (Moon)
- Lavender = right use of power (dawn/dusk)
- Pink = love, integration (dawn/dusk)

Cast the prayer arrow into running water, or plant it upright in the earth in a place where you will not return and it cannot be easily found by others. Once sent out, the prayer arrow is not yours anymore. Release it within 48 hours.

One time, Angeles told the story of learning about prayer arrows. She had visited Central America where she learned about the prayer arrows from an indigenous group there, and had participated in making one. She had to leave almost immediately so packed her prayer arrow in her bag. Upon return to San Francisco, she realized that the 48 hours would be up soon, so she stopped to throw the arrow off the Golden Gate Bridge.

Weeks later, she was attending an event on a boat in the San Francisco bay. She was bored by the actual event and started exploring the boat. The captain noticed her and offered her a tour. When they got to the helm, she saw her prayer arrow on the wall. She asked, "Is there a story about that object?" The captain replied that he had been taking a group to the Farallon Islands for whale watching one day when he saw this colorful object bobbing on the surface. He got a net and fished it out. He said that he had been having very good luck since finding it. Angeles never told him that she had made it, because once released, the prayer arrow is no longer yours.

Prayer Arrow ceremony: February 2014

Present Forward. This phrase means to let go of the past, and live in the present, the only place where you can create your preferred future. Choices are made in the present that affect your future. When people in the circle lapsed into stories of the past, Angeles often gently reminded them to come "present forward" into a problem-solving mode that would shape-shift the past.

Pride. Pride is an unhealthy need to look good and be seen in a certain way (not as we really are). It is a major obstacle to love and authenticity. In order to control how others see us, we may lapse into control or appeasement strategies. Once Angeles said, "pride and grace do not dwell in the same place."

Primal Needs. Every person has at least three of these communal/interpersonal needs: time for myself, quality time in relationships, and time in community. If I don't make time for myself, I am vulnerable to being manipulated out of a sense of duty. These three matched the focus of a vision quest; to contemplate where we are in terms of our work with self, relationships, and community.

Probe. The root of the word "problem" is probe. It means to explore, discover, and stay in curiosity. Therefore, a problem is an invitation to gather more information and begin an exploration process. Probing often involves asking questions.

Psychomythology. This is our nonverbal language, and our past history, plus the symbols and images that help us make meaning of our experience. Angeles said "our psychomythology is greater than our psychopathology." Psyche means logos, or our wisdom nature; mythos means our life dreams and purpose. What images come up in my daydreams? What symbols/images in nature am I consistently drawn to? Collages are an effective way of playing with these images and integrating our experience.

What "P" words speak to you? What is your work at this time?

Q is for Questing

A quest in world literature is an epic journey, a path of discovery. I have learned, though, that daily life can also represent a quest. Angeles helped us see how important the daily practices are to aligning our lives in meaning and authenticity. The *Four Fold Way*™ work is a quest for the authentic life; the *Second Half of Life*™ work is a quest for meaning and integrity as one ages. A vision quest is an experience alone, in silence and stillness in nature. We are constantly and continually in quest of our life dreams.

One year near the end of a vision quest, I had an animal helper ally visitation that summed up my seeds of learning, and I wrote this story as my integration project for the year.

The Quest for the Holy Grail

In June of 2010, Queen Angeles assembled her knights of the Four Fold Way™ to prepare them for a noble quest. She began by ringing Excalibur, the bell of truth, and calling upon the blessings, learnings, mercies, and protections to fortify the fellowship. From Camelot, also known as base camp, the knights set forth on the quest. This is the story of just one of the members of the fellowship, Ser Micalot, who began the quest with great doubt and anxiety, not sure what the Holy Grail looked like, and hoping she would recognize it if she happened to stumble upon it.

Ser Micalot set off on her journey, layered up against the damp chill, and within minutes encountered the first challenge. Hordes of ferocious winged creatures surrounded her, emitting a high-pitched buzz that she feared would drive her insane. But she was well prepared and had protections. A small dose of DEET, and the evil minions sought flesh elsewhere. Exhausted by the first battle, she decided to meditate for guidance before resuming her journey. Three hours later, she awoke, feeling guilty about delaying her journey for so long, but then she remembered her Queen's advice: sleep when your body tells you to, and she felt better.

The next challenge was how to go about finding the Holy Grail. After some reflection, she decided that the most likely place for it to be hidden was in the vast and dark reaches of her own psyche. She needed a map to negotiate this uncharted territory. Where could she find one? As she thought about the problem, her eyes landed on a large spreading black oak tree on the slope above her. The elaborate branching patterns were a perfect match for the vast wilderness in her head. She began to follow a gnarled branch. To her dismay, the branch led to the trunk of the tree where she found a flashing neon light, "**Going down; Enter at your own risk**." The arrow pointed to the ground, and she realized that the path to the Holy Grail was subterranean, through the vast root system of the tree. She shuddered, but was committed to the quest, so she plunged inside the nearest root, clutching her bright orange whistle just in case. Soon she encountered an ancient gnome, barring the way. "NO ONE SHALL PASS LEST THEY TRUTHFULLY ANSWER THE QUESTIONS," he announced in a booming voice.

Fearfully, Ser Micalot inquired, "What questions, good sir?"

"WHY, SPINOZA's QUESTIONS OF COURSE," the gnome replied. Ser Micalot was able to answer with confidence, as all of the fellowship had ample practice with these questions. She was able to pass into the bowels of her psyche, or at least she assumed that's where she was by the smell.

By now, the path was narrowing and she came to a large crossroads with dozens of paths branching off in different directions. She felt a moment of doubt, but then decided to stand in the threshold of each path and listen with her heart. She had faith that her heart would know the way.

On the opening to the first path, she saw a mist shrouded Madonna-like figure in the distance. She looked closer, and the figure began to sing, "Beauty's where you find it, not just where you bump and grind it....Vogue, Vogue, Vogue." That's a good lesson, said her heart, but this is not your path.

At the next threshold, she saw a choir standing at attention. When they noticed her, they began to sing, "You can't always get what you want, but if you try sometimes, you just might find, you get what you need." She marked this path on the map for future exploration, and moved to the next branch.

"You're gonna need an ocean of Calamine lotion," emanated from this one. She hastily stepped back and moved to the next path. The base camp crew had prepared her well to avoid the poison oak.

The beat was loud and pounding from the next threshold and she had to listen closely to discern the words, but finally they became clear, "Ga Ga Ooo la la, Caught in a Bad Romance." She winced and stepped back—past relationships were not today's quest.

The next threshold held a lighter, more wistful sound, "Don't it always seem to go that you don't know what you got til it's gone…"

Ser Micalot stepped out of that one as well, wondering if she had stumbled into the rock and roll hall of fame hell and was doomed to spend eternity listening to the likes of Yummy, Yummy, Yummy, I've got Love in My Tummy. So she approached the next threshold with some trepidation. "I just dropped in to see what condition my condition was in." That's it, that's the path, her heart whispered. Here is the road to the Holy Grail. She stepped across the threshold, leaving her comfort zone behind.

The path was long, steep, full of pitfalls and dark places, and the song whispered seductively in her ears as she traveled,

> "I woke up this mornin' with the sundown shinin' in, I found my mind in a brown paper bag within. I tripped on a cloud and fell-a eight miles high, I tore my mind on a jagged sky, I just dropped in to see what condition my condition was in. (Yeah, yeah, oh-yeah, what condition my condition was in). I pushed my soul in a deep dark hole and then I followed it in. I watched myself crawlin' out as I was a-crawlin' in, I got up so tight I couldn't unwind, I saw so much I broke my mind, I just dropped in to see what condition my condition was in."

The journey was painful at times, but also enlightening and she started feeling her mind, heart, and guts shifting, coming into alignment from the spiritual tune-up she was getting on this voyage.

126

Eventually she rounded a corner and found herself in a peaceful woodlands clearing with filtered sunlight dappling the grass. It looked so inviting, that she dropped down in the soft fragrant grass, listened to the wind stirring the leaves on the tops of the trees and fell asleep. As soon as her body and mind had stilled and she stopped striving, a small dark gray bird with a question mark on its head landed on her left foot and woke her up. She gazed at the beautiful bird in awe, wondering what it was. As if it could read her mind, the bird answered, "I am the Holy Quail."

"What????" she said, "holy quail?"

"Haven't you ever heard of a mis-translation?" the bird replied in a rather snarky tone. "Those 18th century scribes got it all wrong and turned me into a cup! Grail, indeed." The bird seemed to become aware of its tone, shape-shifted, and turned serious again.

"So you see, your quest is not a crusade, or a journey with a roadmap and itinerary. You don't get to your destination by accumulating frequent flyer miles. You cannot slay your dragons with words and thoughts alone. Your journey is at home, inside of yourself. It is the pursuit of wisdom, found in nature's holy temple, with me, The Holy Quail, as your tour guide. Next time you see me, we will work on patience, compassion, and suspending judgment—these are some of your demons."

Suddenly the Quail disappeared and Ser Micalot found herself alone once again in the little clearing feeling energized and fully present. She brought her seeds of learning from the Holy Quail back to the fellowship, and found that each member had experienced a unique journey, and each had brought seeds of wisdom to share with the rest of the fellowship. And they rejoiced, gave thanks, and went home mindfully, staying in nature's rhythm, medium to slow, to continue the sacred quest for their life dreams.

What are the seeds of learning from your latest quest? What creative projects help you to integrate your learning? How have helper allies aided your quest for authencity?

"Q" Glossary

Qualms. These are the doubts that stem from the critical doubting mind, not the wisdom voice. If we have doubts, we should not take action. It is important to wait for clarity, or our actions will come from reactivity, not the inner wisdom voice.

Questions. Asking good questions that take people out of their roles and identities and to the heart of deeper learning is the skill of a good teacher. "If we have a question, we also have the answer," Angeles would say. The entire *Four Fold Way*™ program, and all of Angeles' teachings really, are based on asking questions. We can question ourselves to identify hidden patterns and old stories, and we can question others, rather than give unsolicited advice, and help them discover their own truth. Questions lead the way to the answers.

> "If others tell us something we make assumptions, and if they don't tell us something we make assumptions to fulfill our need to know and to replace the need to communicate. Even if we hear something and we don't understand we make assumptions about what it means and then believe the assumptions. We make all sorts of assumptions because we don't have the courage to ask questions."
> — Miguel Ruiz, *The Four Agreements.*

Quadrants. Dividing a paper into four equal quadrants represents the plus sign, a universal sign of integration and balance. Angeles often had us examine quadrants, like the life transitions (work, relationship, health, finances in the four quadrants, with our inner work in the center). In my 2012 journal, I found a reference to Angeles describing Island peoples drawing a plus sign in the sand and reflecting on the following four quadrants at the beginning of a new year.

What are my hopes this year? What is inspiring or uplifting me?	What are my fears going into this new year?
What are my strengths?	What are my challenges? (where do I need to grow?)

She said you should have someone witness each of these rituals.

- The hopes are celebrated.
- The fears are thrown into a fire.
- The strengths are tied to water—flexible and fluid. They are put in a cup, named, and then you drink to them.
- The challenges are the invitation to grow.

If we have more than three items in any quadrant, we may be in overload. Fewer than three, we are not stretching ourselves.

Quiet. "In the quiet mind, all things are possible." Angeles talked a lot about the value of silence and slowing down to nature's rhythm so that we can still the active mind and access the heart. Healing work needs a slower pace and quiet. She also described the wisdom voice as a clear, but quiet voice within.

What "Q" words speak to you? What is your work at this time?

R is for Raven

Angeles' spirit animal is the raven. Someone who lived in the same town as Angeles once told me that she knew when Angeles was home, because a flock of ravens was always in the trees in her yard if she was present. When Patrick O'Neill organized a workshop to honor her teaching and transition, we had a visitation of dozens of ravens, gathering in the trees outside our meeting room. They assailed us with a raucous song of welcome and appeared to approve of our gathering.

According to Ted Andrew's *Animal Speak*, the raven is associated with magic, shapeshifting, and creation. In many indigenous cultures, raven plays an important part in the mythology, as an omen, a messenger from the gods, as a trickster. They are intelligent, playful, use tools, are fearless. Raven is the bird of birth and death. Or as Andrews noted "with raven, human and animal spirits intermingle and become as one." He also noted, "If raven comes into your life, expect magic."

After a vision quest held on the first anniversary after her passing, and after several significant encounters with raven, I wrote this piece.

Quoth the Raven

The Raven, the dark and chilling tale by Edgar Allen Poe, is one of the world's most recognized poems. In this story, raven is harbinger of evil and death who comes in the dark of night when fears that were submerged by the light of day now re-emerge and intensify. The powerful words of the poem evoke a spine-chilling fear, symbolized by the raven. But what if Edgar Allen Poe had met Angeles Arrien, whose spirit animal is raven? This raven was not evil, or haunting, but wickedly intelligent, funny, and wise. This raven communicated a message of heart and meaning, standing for and by your values, speaking your truth clearly, and living in integrity and authenticity. So, if Mr. Poe had experienced this raven and had sat in the healing circle with Angeles, his poem would have been very different, perhaps something like this:

Once upon a dawn so dreamy while I bathed in light so gleamy,
Over many a quaint and curious volume of forgotten lore,
While I nodded, nearly napping, suddenly there came a tapping,
As of some one gently rapping, rapping at my chamber door.
"Tis some visitor," I muttered, "tapping at my chamber door-
        Only this, and nothing more."

Ah, distinctly I remember she declared "see you in September"
And each ancestor spirit beamed patiently by the door
Eagerly awaiting assignment, while happily I sought to borrow
From my books to prepare for tomorrow,
A preferred future brimming with ancient lore
        More of this, forever more.

And the silken, gay, rustling of each dawn's life dream
Thrilled me---filled me with fantastic visions never seen before
So that now to fill the heart so full and strong, I stood repeating
"Tis some visitor entreating entrance at my chamber door
        Only some important stranger—this and nothing more."

Presently my warrior grew stronger, hesitating then no longer
"Sir," said I, "or Madam, truly your forgiveness I implore;
But the fact is I was napping, and so gently you came rapping,
And so faintly you came tapping, tapping at my chamber door,
That I scarce was sure I heard you"- here I opened the round door;-
        The dawn with secrets to share and so much more.

Deep into the dim morn peering, long I stood there wondering, hearing
waking visionary dreams no mortal ever dared to dream before;
But the sweet territory of silence was unbroken,
and the stillness gave no token,
And the only word there spoken was the whispered "don't go back to
sleep "
This I whispered, and mystery murmured back, "don't go back to sleep"-
        Merely this, and nothing more.

What are your experiences with Raven? Do you have a spirit
animal? How did it come to you?

"R" Glossary

Rattle Work. The rattle represents cleansing work, as it mimics the sound of rain. It symbolizes purification, soul retrieval, and empowerment. It is a tool of the warrior and can be used for problem-solving, sealing your sides, calling in the ancestors, and general cleansing work.

Reactivity. This is when we get triggered by something in the present that brings up a painful memory of the past or a fear of the future. We move into an emotional state of anger, frustration, grief, guilt, or fear which floods us and clouds our ability to access the wisdom voice. When in a reactive mode, we should ask for more time and space before we respond or make any decisions. We are not reliable in the state of reactivity. We have a responsibility to feel these emotions, but then move beyond them. To stay in a reactive state for too long is an example of indulging. A way to move beyond reactivity is to engage curiosity and a healthy detachment to examine what triggered the feelings. If we do not attach to a feeling, it passes fairly quickly.

Rebel. One of the shadow qualities is rebellion against authority, or rules. Often our rebellion hurts us and we behave in a way contrary to our well-being, such as resisting our own learning and growth.

Rebirth. After every major life transition, we can be reborn and become a better, more honorable, more authentic person. All we have to do is let go of the past and our old stories that no longer serve us. Death and rebirth are continually occurring processes through-out our life times.

Recognition. This is another of the arms of love. We recognize (and acknowledge, validate, and appreciate) our loved ones, and every one and thing around us to manifest more love in the world.

Reflection. This is a powerful tool for making change. First we have to pay attention to our experiences, and reflect on how a current situation fits in with old patterns or older experiences. Reflection can lead to insights that help us see how to change. Time in silence and solitude in nature can foster reflection. Reflection is a tool for integration.

Regret versus Remorse. There is a difference between these two concepts. According to Angeles, remorse means to feel so bad about the pain we caused another that we are motivated to take action so that we never let it happen again. Regret, on the other hand, is a paralyzing brew of shame and guilt that never moves to action or change. Angeles often said that the greatest regret is love unexpressed.

Relationships. Angeles always said "relationship is a rigorous spiritual practice." She noted that we have to pay attention to three things: my dream, your dream, and our dream. The last is a true collaboration and mutual process of creating a shared life that honors and respects limits and boundaries and allows each person to fulfill their own dreams as well. Five qualities that foster relationships are: honesty, respect, trust, openness, and vulnerability. We need to ask ourselves, "Who am I in relationship? Am I myself?"

In small group activities over the years, Angeles asked participants to engage with some of these questions about relationship:

- What is the heart of my relationship work now?
- How have I improved?
- What are my patterns?
- Where do I hold curiosity in terms of my relationships?
- What relationships are currently inspiring me?
- Who is the most difficult person in my life now?
- Where is there the greatest flow in current relationships?
- Who is new in my life? (shows me new aspects of myself)
- What are the undiscussables in my relationship?
- What am I avoiding or fearing in my relationship?

Resources. A daily practice around resources is to ask yourself each morning, "What is the resource that will best support my wellbeing today?" It might be patience, flexibility, trust, integrity, humor, courage, and so on. Then do a ritual with the six directions found in all cultures. Imagine that you are putting that needed resource:

- Before me (in the future)
- Behind me (in the past)
- Above me (anchored in the heavens)
- Below me (anchored in the earth)
- To the left of me (in all my relationships)
- To the right of me (in all my actions today)

In other words, the resource is within me and all around me ("everywhere now"). Angeles described our resources as our "internal garments."

Respect. The core of this word means to "look again." We need both self-respect and respect for others. In regards to self, if our behaviors are aligned with our core values and we follow through on our commitments, we can develop self-trust. If we know what qualities are unshakeable, and what resources we can draw on in times of stress, we build our self respect. In terms of other people, respect is the wisdom and obligation to consider another person's perspective and entertain the idea that we might be wrong or misled, and re-consider our assumptions. Respect is honoring another person's limits and boundaries, and listening deeply to their words with the intention of understanding their perspective.

In my 2012 journal, Angeles offered three areas where we can reflect on how we are respecting our roots. She said we are often too eager to forget the past and not honor the contribution that it made to our lives. We can honor:

1. Our parents. How can we honor and respect them even if they caused us pain and harm? Can we show respect even if we disagree with some of the things they did?
2. Our religion of origin: what did it provide as a foundation or root for our early lives? Even if I rejected that religion later, what lessons did I learn in youth that aided my development?
3. Our culture of origin: what lessons have I learned from my racial/ethnic, national origin, or geographic-based culture?

Right Placement. When we are in a job that lets our gifts and talents shine, in a relationship where we are appreciated and loved, and live in a place that makes us feel safe and protected, we are in right placement.

Right Timing. Sometimes we know the right thing to say at the right time, or are at the best time in our life to make some change or launch into a new phase of life. This phrase, from Buddhism, indicates the importance of knowing the right time. It is not the right time if we feel doubts, confusion, or are reactive (angry, hurt, in pain).

Righteousness. This is a fixed viewpoint that does not leave room for change and stems from a need to be right or a tendency toward victimhood. We have to give it up in order to solve a problem.

Ritual. According to Angeles, we have lost a great deal of value in our lives by dropping the rituals of the life course that are still practiced in many indigenous cultures. These rituals help us to come to the present moment, to foster reflection, integrate, and celebrate life transitions. A ritual can be as simple as lighting a candle every morning, or practicing a more elaborate ritual like a prayer arrow ceremony or a tobacco trap. They can be rituals that mark the passage of time, like doing something new on the day of your birth every month.

Rivers of Life. This is one of the tracking tools Angeles often used. We can track daily, or by season, where we found:

- Inspiration (those things that bring us hope),
- Challenge (an invitation to grow),
- Surprise (how we handle the unexpected that shows us our flexibility or attachments),
- Love (where we have the capacity to be touched and moved by life. "Love cross-pollinates like pollen and stings like bee").

What "R" words speak to you? What is your work at this time?

S is for Silence

Angeles often started her group sessions with this request, "Let us go into the sweet territory of silence." Silence helped to ground the group and put us into a more reflective, contemplative mode. It changed the energy in the room. A moment of silence helps ease the transition from one activity to another.

When I was younger, I was more focused on silence in terms of feeling silenced. I had experiences when my voice was not valued, and I felt I had no right to speak. It took me years to learn to stand up for myself and others and speak my truth. I learned there is a big difference between being silenced and choosing silence as a spiritual practice.

As I have aged, I have grown to crave silence on a regular basis; I need a time when I can really think or alternatively, suspend thought for a little while and just enjoy natural sounds that are a portal to the wisdom voice. I ran across this description of silence in an essay I read recently:

> "The roots of our English term 'silence' sink down through the language in multiple directions. Among the word's antecedents is the Gothic verb *anasilan*, a word that denotes the wind dying down, and the Latin *desinere*, a word meaning 'stop.' Both of these etymologies suggest the way that silence is bound up with the idea of interrupted action. The pursuit of silence, likewise, is dissimilar from most other pursuits in that it generally begins with a surrender of the chase, the abandonment of efforts to impose our will and vision on the world. Not only is it about standing still; with rare exceptions, the pursuit of silence seems initially to involve a step backward from the tussle of life." (George Prochnick, 2011, *In pursuit of silence*).

I think Prochnick captures part of a trilogy of silence, stillness, and solitude. He notes that we need to be still to appreciate the silence. I would add that solitude is needed for deep silence. The combination of solitude, stillness, and silence is potent, particularly when spent out in nature. My favorite place to experience this powerful combination is at the beach.

"Let us look for secret things somewhere in the world on the blue shore of silence." --Pablo Neruda

One of the greatest values of spending time in solitude in nature is the experience of silence. In our everyday lives, we are surrounded by unnatural noise; traffic, construction, fire engine sirens, dogs barking, music blaring from cars as they pass by, conversations of other people on the bus and in restaurants, or the neighbor's TV or stereo. Most of all, there is that incessant chatter in our own heads, the internal voice that never shuts up. Nature is full of sound as well, but in solitude, the absence of the unnatural sounds allows us to hear the natural—wind rustling the grasses, the singing sands, roaring waves, tree branches creaking in the wind, and the multitude of different bird calls. These natural sounds promote a sense of inner stillness. Mark Coleman (*Alive in the Wild*) noted that *"silence is the doorway to the mystery, to the sacred. It is in silence that we can feel the essence of things"* (p. 148).

Most religious and spiritual traditions value silence as the doorway to the sacred, as access to the soul. One of the proverbs in the old testament Bible noted, "closing one's lips makes a person wise." It implies that listening deepens wisdom more than speaking. Silence allows us to access the inner world, without the noisy distractions of the outer world. But silence is a rare commodity in today's world.

In *A Square Inch of Silence*, Gordon Hempton, an acoustic ecologist, recounted his search for natural silence in the United States. He studied the impact of noise on human and animal life, finding evidence of the devastating effect of man-made noise. For example, noise has been particularly hard on songbirds, because they must sing louder, expending more energy, and making them more vulnerable to predators. At least one-fourth of all bird species in the U.S. are on the decline. Dolphins in China's Yangtze River are nearly extinct, mostly because of the noise of shipping traffic.

In humans, noise pollution is associated with higher levels of aggression and a decline in helping behavior toward others. Road traffic noise has been linked to cardiovascular disease. There are over 5000 research articles that show detrimental effects of noise, likening it to second hand smoke.

Hempton's travels revealed only a handful of places in the entire U.S. with natural quiet, defined as an interval of more than 15 minutes without an intrusion of man-made noise. Our national parks have only about five minute intervals of natural quiet during daylight hours. Silence should be on the endangered list along with the California condor. Whenever we can find those rare moments, we need to cherish our time spent in "the sweet territory of silence." Perhaps I am so drawn to the beach because the roar of the waves drowns out any man-made sound, such as an airplane overhead. I can ground myself in that rhythmic sound of waves spilling over, crashing, and receding. As the song says, Silence is golden.

What is your relationship to silence? Do you deliberately practice silence on a regular basis?

"S" Glossary

Sacrifice. This word comes from the root word, to make sacred. Mostly Angeles talked about sacrificing the false self, allowing the authentic self to show. Walking meditation helps to reclaim the authentic self. Sometimes when we give away pieces of ourselves and put others before our own needs, we falsely label this as sacrifice. Angeles always stated that our own self-care must come first.

Say What Is So, When It's So. This is one of the principles of integrity in speaking: speak from the heart at the time it needs to be said. Don't wait until later or hold back for fear of offending some one. This is a principle of addressing issues as they arise instead of deflecting or avoiding. Conflict avoiders are challenged in practicing this principle, even though if they did engage in it, the chances of conflict would be reduced significantly.

Scarcity. This is an unnatural state of feeling deprived, and causes fear and greed. The natural state is one of abundance of spirit. Abundance is having enough to meet our needs and to share with others. Resources like love and compassion are infinite and abundant.

Seasons. Each season is attached to an archetype and holds different types of activities for personal growth:

- Spring (healer). This is a collective time of reflection, death/rebirth, and letting go so that I can truly be free. The focus is on self-care. The spring is time of ancestral and family healing as well as self-healing.
- Summer (visionary). This is the time of renewal, regeneration, when everything in nature comes into its fullness. It's the time to sacrifice the false self, the parts that edit, rehearse, perform, control, and tries to look good (ego). Summer shows us where we are susceptible to temptations. The middle of the year is a good time to course-correct. August is the month of revelation in northern African Berber tribes, and the Irish call it the month of surprises. Jung said that summer represents the midpoint between birth and death.

- Fall (teacher). This is the only season with two simultaneous processes: 1) harvesting from the seeds we planted earlier in the year; and 2) letting go to make room for new growth. The winds of fall can sometimes make us feel scattered, but we can use the wind within us (the breath) to bring us back to ourselves to conserve our energies.
- Winter (warrior). This is the time to work on rigor, discipline, and excellence. We need a willingness to make mistakes and learn from them, take time to practice vulnerability, and work on reducing our self-critic. We may hibernate—take time for ourselves to reflect and conserve our energy.

Secrets. Secrets cut our power in half because it takes much energy to conceal and we can become controlled by fear of exposure. Secrets are a source of shame, guilt and fear, and not the same as privacy. Privacy carries none of those negative feelings. In some Native American groups, secrets are spoken once every five years, ending with "and from this day I no longer live a divided life." Another strategy is to tell a large boulder or tree of the secret, and then release it forever. It is inappropriate to saddle our friends or family with our secrets.

Seeding. This is a process of sharing what we learned from an experience, rather than merely telling the story. The story can take us away from the seeds of learning and start to have a life of its own; the seeds hold the ingredients we need to integrate our experience. Seeds are the lessons we need to consider for reflection and integration, detached from the story.

Self-Critic. Often, the self-critic is the most negative voice in our lives. It nags, cajoles, and berates us for things that come from social conditioning; all the "shoulds." It is not the voice of integrity or wisdom. Curiosity is the antidote to the critic. Ask yourself daily, "Is my curiosity greater than my criticality?" One day, I wrote a mock want ad:

> Wanted: Full-time wisdom voice to take over internal operations from an over-powering self-critic. Qualifications: a compassionate truth-teller with strong skills in detachment and discernment. Advanced training

141

in the FourFold Way™ highly desirable. Doubting, judgmental voices need not apply.

Self-trust. The three planks of trust are trust in self, trust in others, and trust in the circumstances. Self-trust is challenging for many of us, particularly if our false-self system is still intact and we cannot listen to our hearts.

Self-Care. Angeles stressed how important it is for us to care for ourselves. We are no good to others if we neglect our own health, emotional, and other needs. Self-care is not an indulgence; it is a necessity. We need to attend to diet/nutrition, physical activity, rest, and owning our own power. In most spiritual traditions, the body is considered the temple, and we must treat it with the utmost respect as our physical container. If we exceed our physical limits and boundaries, the body will tackle us and force us to pay attention. When we live fully in our bodies, we are embodied and our authentic nature is visible to others.

Shadow. This idea comes from Jung. Angeles pointed out that all good qualities can have a shadow side if taken to an extreme— that is why balance across all the archetypes is so important. If we over-identify with only one archetype, we can easily lapse into shadow characteristics. A shadow side of love is giving ourselves away; a shadow side to sufficiency is pride. A shadow of patience is rigidity and control issues. A common shadow side of the healer is the tendency to try to "fix" others. Shadow traits are qualities that we ignore, avoid, or project on others rather than reclaim and embrace. We often cannot see them directly, but they manifest indirectly in myth, symbols, and behavior patterns. Sometimes we catch a glimpse of them in ourselves or dislike them in other people but do not recognize that it is because we have these traits ourselves. We need to start a process of befriending the shadow and reclaiming those lost pieces of ourselves (soul retrieval work). Deep healing occurs when we face the fears that we hoped to keep hidden. When we shed the secrets, we can transform. Shadows are not always negative things; sometimes they are positive qualities that we have not yet claimed, like courage and patience. At the end of this section, you will find an assessment of the common shadow sides for each of the four archetypes.

In 2011, we did a meditation process to reflect on the shadow side. It has these three steps:

142

1. Focus on the positive quality you want to consider (example; compassion). It is a resource that you can draw on at any time.
2. Look at the situation that challenges this resource (what takes you out of compassion and into judgment or hatred). Pay attention to the physical sensations, the emotions, and the thoughts that this elicits. Track the triggers and practice breathing through the situation.
3. Remind yourself of the positive quality and consider how you can bring it into this challenging situation. Remember that you can do things differently the next time.

Snarky. This was Angeles' term for the way we behave when we are having a bad day or behaving in a way that is "less than becoming."

Softening. This is one of the four tracking tools that Angeles like to use at the end of a season or year (along with deepening, opening, and strengthening). To soften means to smooth out our rough edges and to become more gentle with ourselves and others.

Solitude. This is the productive state of being alone, as opposed to being lonely. Every human being needs time to reflect and integrate their experiences, and time spent in silence and solitude creates the most productive crucible for that work. Angeles helped that process by providing a vision quest every year, with 2 nights and three days alone and in silence in nature.

Soul Retrieval. This refers to the process of retrieving lost pieces of the self and reclaiming all the shadow, traumas, and past experiences until we become whole again. Winter is a good time for strengthening and re-gathering the self.

Spinoza's Questions. These questions are a tracking tool for recognizing what is working in our lives. When we focus on what is working, we are better able to see and handle what is not working. The questions are:

• Who or what inspired me today?
• Where did I experience joy, comfort, and ease today?

- What made me happy? (not who; what made me happy that is not relationally dependent?)

Standing (for and by). This is a quality of the warrior: this part of us knows what our core values are and stands by them. We are firm in our convictions.

Standing Meditation. Standing meditation helps us to strengthen our values so that we can stand by and for them. Standing meditation for an hour a day will develop leadership skills by increasing self-respect, decreasing conflict avoidance, and opening the body to guidance. When the body is uncrossed and open, the wisdom voice is more likely to emerge. Standing meditation is a practice of the warrior.

Story. Angeles often talked about the dangers of repeating old stories, to ourselves and to others. People often use stories for negative bonding, not a great way to forge a relationship. In addition, we get lots of positive attention and sympathy from the story, so upon the next telling it gets embellished a little. The story takes on a life of its own, and keeps the old wounds from healing. We often hang on to old stories about ourselves that are simply not current and hold us back from being fully present and authentic.

Strengthening. Along with softening, deepening, and opening, we can track what strengthens in our nature over time. When we strengthen, we build up our personhood and develop better capacity for patience, flexibility, courage, and other resources that help us in life.

Success. In my 2010 journal, I found reference to the six steps to success from a cross-cultural perspective. They include:

1. Be disciplined. Take the next step; do not push or hold back, but be disciplined to go step-by-step.
2. Be flexible. Successful people are early adopters and adapters. The form always changes, so we must be flexible to accommodate these changes. Where we have habits or routines reflect our attachments.
3. Successful people love what they do. Follow what has heart and meaning.

144

4. Successful people value integrity, honesty, and authenticity. They are truth-tellers and speak up against injustice.
5. Successful people are effective communicators. They say what is so when it's so, but also in the right time and place. Their words, body language, and actions are aligned.
6. They have a sense of humor. Humor sparks creativity and productivity. High spiritual leaders are flexible, funny, and don't push or hold back.

In small groups, Angeles asked us to share our top three characteristics and discuss which areas need work. We can examine these six qualities in terms of self, relationship, and collective/community work, and take an action to strengthen one of these every day.

Sufficiency. In 2005, Angeles presented this definition of sufficiency: "a healthy allegiance and expression of self-worth, stronger than past experience, self-criticism, self-doubts, and external circumstances." Sufficiency is knowing that we have the resources to handle whatever is before us, and stepping up to do it. When we doubt or let fear take over, we lose our power. When we are in sufficiency, it is not a false confidence. There is no inflation or deflation, but a trust in our true gifts and talents. Angeles was fond of quoting Eleanor Roosevelt: "no one can make me feel inferior unless I agree to it."

Another gem that comes from my journal in 2008 is "insufficiency lives in the vortex between ego and the self-critic." The ego focuses on looking good and the self-critic doubts that we can do whatever we need to do. When feeling insufficient, it is important to identify the one quality that I can trust absolutely, and ground myself in that quality. Sufficiency in one area is transferable; it fosters sufficiency in other areas as well. In my 2010 notes, I wrote "the external world cannot fill the inner holes." Some questions that help us to build and strengthen our sufficiency include:

- What is a gift/strength that I can absolutely rely on?
- What do I trust and respect about myself?
- Where have I been the most inspired and challenged this year?

145

- Who and what do I allow to trigger my insecurities? What are the actions that I can take to interrupt that?

Surprise. Angeles often quoted John Donaghue for this: "I would like to live my life like a river, carried by the surprise of its own unfolding." How we handle surprises, or the unexpected, shows us where we are flexible.

Symbols. Symbols help us to understand our world, and send us messages that help us grow. Jung said that symbols are the psychological mechanism for transformation. It is important to pay attention to what symbols we are drawn to, and try to understand what message they have to tell us. Three symbolic figures that Angeles mentioned several times over the years include those that appear in many folk tales of journeys. These figures appear on the bridge or on the path at crossings:

- The veiled woman is a symbol of that which is emerging but not fully revealed yet. She is a lesson in trust and faith.
- The skeleton is a symbol of sacrifice and a reminder to come back to our authentic nature (our bones). The skeleton symbolizes sacrificing the false self, a necessary step on life's journey. It reminds us to stay connected to our wish bone, back bone, hollow little bone, and funny bone.
- The helping ally or ancestor appears to remind us to stay connected them to them during our transition. They can support us in the life journey.

If we pay attention to the symbols, we are better prepared for the future, or as Rilke put it, "the future enters us long before we are aware of it." Symbols are a sneak preview.

Synchronicity. There are no coincidences; when something appears to be significant, it probably contains a message that you should not ignore. Synchronicities are trying to get your attention. We can pay attention to the symbols and coincidences that give us clues as to our future.

What "S" words speak to you? What is your work at this time?

Shadow Assessment:

How true of you are these statements at this time in your life?
Warrior Shadows
W1. I rebel against authority just for the sake of rebellion.
W2. I have issues with authority figures even when there is no specific reason for it.
W3. I hide or hold back my best work.
W4. I prefer to work behind the scenes rather than be recognized for my contribution.
W5. I tend to latch onto more powerful people and ride their coattails.
Healer Shadows
H1. I get caught up in drama, feeding on the energy of it.
H2. I cannot bring a task to completion until it is "perfect."
H3. I have a great need to know everything that is going on.
H4. I tend to focus on what is not working rather than what it working.
H5. I am easily bored.
Visionary Shadows
V1. I edit my thoughts and speech rather than speak my truth.
V2. I hide my true opinion.
V3. I have lost my sense of humor.
V4. I give up parts of myself to get acceptance, approval, or keep the peace.
V5. I get over-identified with my own point of view.
Teacher Shadows
T1. I stubbornly stick to one position rather than be open to alternatives.
T2. I find myself judging others.
T3. I sometimes say things at the wrong time or place.
T4. I try to get control over situations.
T5. I often feel confused about the right action to take.

T is for Trust

*"None of us knows what might happen even the next minute, yet still
we go forward. Because we trust. Because we have Faith."*
— *Paulo Coelho,*

The three planks of trust are trust in self, trust in others, and trust
in circumstances. When we individuate from others (first parents,
later significant others or children), we are learning self-trust and
responsibility. Trust is the foundation for all other resources; it is
never in the past, but always in "present-forward" mode. Trust is
embodied and resides in the belly, supported by heart and head.

In one session with Angeles (winter 2008), we held a "council of
trust." In groups of 3-4, we explored these questions that focused
on cultivating our self-trust:

- Where am I visible and where am I hiding in my life?
- Where do I have high needs for approval or acceptance?
- Where am I conflict avoidant?
- Where do I stand behind my own gifts, talents, and experience?
- What can I absolutely trust about myself?

One session got me thinking about my own relationship to trust.
Angeles said if I get into a processing mode and over-analyze a
situation, I have no trust in myself. I spend so much time in my
head, analyzing situations, going over pros and cons, and second-
guessing my decisions. I think this may be the shadow side of a
well-developed intellect. As a university professor, I was trained
to use my analytical thinking skills to solve problems. It is an asset
in my work, but becomes a shadow sometimes when I apply the
same processes to a relationship or a spiritual task. Those require
different skill sets.

Angeles proposed four ways to build trust in relationships:

1. Give enough context to let others know your intentions.
   Verbalize the cause and consequences of our actions and
   make sure everyone is on the same page. Use
   paraphrasing and summarizing of what others say to
   achieve clarity.

2. Be consistent and reliable: do what you say you will do.
3. Be congruent: make sure your words, actions, and body language all give the same message. Say what you mean.
4. If misunderstandings occur, offer genuine apology and set new agreements. Or accept a genuine apology and forgive.

Trust is in the middle way; too much space and too little space both threaten the sense of trust and safety in a relationship. Being too general in your speech and being over-analytical both threaten trust. Situations with high gossip, politics, and building allegiances behind other's backs are not trustworthy.

Two tools to build self-trust include meditation and silent reflection/contemplation. When we focus on what is working, rather than only on what is not working, we find the transferable skills that build our self-confidence. This takes careful tracking so we know what is working, and what qualities we possess that are totally trustworthy.

In my 2005 journal, I found a list of communication skills that can build or re-build trust after a conflict or misunderstanding.

1. Making promises that are concrete and specific and following through with actions.
2. Making commitments (longer-term than promises). Swearing an oath of allegiance.
3. Making agreements. Being clear about what I will do.
4. Acknowledging: validating the other person(s) and recognizing their contributions.
5. Apologizing when needed; this is an act of responsibility that states my role in causing harm and promises action to prevent the harm from happening again.

Where do you have trust in yourself? What situations take you out of self-trust?

"T" Glossary

Tarot. One of Angeles' first books was about her unique spin on interpretation of the tarot, and she continued to teach tarot classes through much of her life. Her approach was to use the cards for self-reflection rather than fortune telling, and she blended numerology, astrology, the Tibetan Book of the Living, and many religious/spiritual traditions into her interpretations of the cards.

One of my favorite stories was about how she discovered the tarot. She was a graduate student in anthropology at Berkeley when a famous Egyptologist gave some rare books to the library. She went to study them one day, and when she opened one of the books, a card fell out. It had all these interesting symbols and numbers on it; images that cut across many cultures and religions. She asked the librarian what it was, and the woman took it from her hand and tore it in half, saying that it was a tarot card and did not belong there. Angeles waited until the librarian left the room for a brief period, then retrieved the card from the waste-basket and taped it back together. She had been studying cross-cultural symbols and this card fascinated her. This began years of work with the tarot and developing her own unique system of interpreting the cards. She did thousands of readings to validate her system.

The tarot deck consists of 78 cards:
- 22 archetypes, or general principles for living (major arcana);
- 16 royalty cards that teach us about relationships; and
- 40 minor arcana that give us information about our mental life/beliefs (swords), our emotional states (cups), our challenges (wands), and the outer world (disks).

Of the 13 challenges, six are in the mind. The four suits also show some similarities to the Myers-Briggs characteristics: swords relate to thinking; cups to feeling; wands to intuition; and disks to sensing.

Angeles often recommended pulling a card each morning and reflecting on its meaning throughout the day.

Task Line. When working in a group, there are always two parallel lines: the relationship line that expresses how people treat and view each other, and the task line, or the job to be accomplished. Angeles believed that both lines had to be tended to for a group to be successful. She proposed that work groups should be no larger than 5 people to be efficient.

Teaching Stories.   Angeles often shared folk tales from indigenous peoples that had lessons about being authentic, or telling the truth, or being patient. In the circle, I learned about creating stories for myself that helped to solidify the learning, but putting the Four Fold Way ™ concepts into stories that were already familiar to me. This one came after a vision quest where I had a flashback to the Wizard of Oz, one of my favorite movies as a child.

Archetypes in the Emerald City

Once upon a time, a timid meek girl, let's call her Dorothy, was strolling down a six foot rut she had worn in the dusty country lane, trailed by her faithful helper ally, Toto. Unexpectedly, a disembodied voice spoke to her. "Dorothy, what is calling to be healed in your nature at this time?" Dorothy whirled around, looking for the source of the voice and not finding it, addressed her response to the heavens. "I'm doing just fine, thank you very much." She quickly forgot the incident as she meandered home, until another event shook her awake from her stupor. For the umpteenth time that year, Toto reverted to her shadow passive-aggressive side, and peed on Miss Elvira Gulch's flower-bed, putting the older woman into a rage. Dorothy, as usual, hid behind Auntie Em's skirts when Miss Gulch appeared at the gate.

But this day was different, being on the cusp between winter and spring. Auntie Em did not stand up for Dorothy, but demanded that she take responsibility. Dorothy let her conflict avoidance take over and she fled from home with Toto in tow, planning to run away. Very soon her fear overwhelmed her, and she decided to go back home. But as we know, there is our plan and the mystery's plan, and today the mystery prevailed. A big wind blew Dorothy out of the plains and plunked her down in the fog of San Francisco. Dazed she looked around, and as the fog dissipated, she found herself on a sandy beach in a strange and unfamiliar landscape. She exclaimed, "Toto, I don't think we are in Iowa anymore. We have escaped the wicked Miss Gulch!" But we all know that troubles keep showing up at our gate if we don't address them, so sure enough, Miss Gulch, now manifest as the Wicked Witch rode in on her broomstick and cackled in her best critics mocking voice, "I'll get you and your little dog, too. Give me your power, my pretty."

Stunned and shaking with fear, Dorothy realized that the Witch was pointing to her red shoes, where all her gifts and talents seemed to have been lodged during her flight in the cyclone. The Witch reached for the shoes, but they appeared to have very strong limits and boundaries and repelled the Witch's approach. When the Witch flew off in a rage, a flock of talking seagulls surrounded Dorothy, telling her that there was a wondrous and wise Wizard in the land who could help her get back home. When she asked how to find the Wizard, they sang in unison, "Follow the Golden Gate Bridge."

Dorothy set out on her journey to find the Wizard, but soon came to a fork in the road and stopped in confusion—Which way led to the bridge? As she waited for clarity to come, a Teacher, in the guise of a gangly Scarecrow suddenly appeared and helped her align her heart, head, and gut to make the right decision. They proceeded down the road together and began to climb a steep hill. The top of the hill was obscured in a dense fog, and Dorothy and the Scarecrow had to trust Toto's acute dog senses to navigate. Toto led them to a Tin Man, rusted in place by the moist air. When they oiled the Tin Man's joints, they found that he was an archetype of the heart, a healer who helped them find meaning in their quest for the Wizard. The Tin Man helped Dorothy see that her conflict avoidance had damaged her relationships with Auntie Em and with Toto, because she appeased Toto instead of asking for accountability and responsibility. The Tin Man joined them in their journey, which next took them thru a eucalyptus grove, fragrant, but dark and menacing. They linked arms and chanted "Shadows and talents and gifts, oh my." A large figure loomed ahead on the path, blocking their way. They turned to run away, but stopped when the huge figure hunkered down to pet Toto. The figure turned out to be a noble lion, king of the forest, a leader among all the creatures great and small. The gentle Warrior Lion joined the others and they made their way onto the Golden Gate Bridge.

Just as they reached the middle of the mighty orange bridge, the Wicked Witch rode in again on her broomstick, testing the wisdom of the Scarecrow, the heart of the Tin Man, the courage of the Lion, and the integrity of Dorothy. Only Toto seemed unaffected by the Witch's menacing presence. The Witch sneered at the small group, who huddled together for support. "You are still missing something very important, my little pretties, I will get those slippers yet!" and she flew off, her taunting laughter ringing in the company's ears.

They continued across the bridge and down a winding road to the Emerald City of Sausalito to a street called Bridgeway, where they found the home of the beloved Wizard. The Wizard, a petite but powerful woman, was a Visionary. She took a long look at Dorothy and told her the truth without blame or judgment, "Ah, you have been behaving in a manner that is less than becoming." She recognized that Dorothy had not yet integrated her learnings, and gave her another task to complete. The test was sinisterly simple—practice the tools daily until she could obtain the Witch's broomstick as a symbol of honorable closure.

The long and hazardous journey to confront the Witch involved the Scarecrow helping Dorothy find a wisdom path of detachment, the Tin Man showing Dorothy the power of love and relationship to conquer all, the Lion showing her how to stand in her integrity and face her fears, and the Wizard revealing the big picture of how these were all related to Dorothy's life dream. When Dorothy finally confronted the Wicked Witch, Dorothy became larger not smaller, the Witch melted away, and her broomstick merged with Dorothy's spine, giving her a strong backbone. The Scarecrow, Tin Man, Lion, and Wizard merged together in the ruby slippers that brought Dorothy home to herself, in the City by the Bay. Oh, and Toto, too.

Testing Our Relationships. Angeles believed that love should not be tested. When we are in fear, we test our relationships. We may push and prod the other to see how they respond to certain situations or scenarios rather than let the relationship unfold as it will. The two fears that underlie most relationships are fear of abandonment and a fear of entrapment. Many of us have both of these fears and sometimes they alternate in a "push-pull" fashion.

Thoughts. Angeles often pointed out the challenges with our capacity to think, and hence, to over-think. In my 2011 journal, I wrote this quote. I'm not sure if it is an Angeles original or from some other source: "Thoughts are just our guests—don't invite them to be roommates." When our thoughts turn to the looping old stories, over-analyzing, comparing, competing, or judging, we are taken out of our authenticity.

Time-Traveling. When you are not in the present moment, you are time-traveling to the past or the future. Often this happens in conversations with others, when words or emotions trigger some memory or fear that sends us out of the present moment. We also time-travel much of the day in our daydreams. Many of the tools that Angeles provided were ways to get current and stay in the present.

Tracking. Angeles offered a number of different tracking tools that help people to stay awake and pay attention. Here are a few examples:

- Were have I strengthened, opened, deepened, and softened? (can be tracked to different time periods: today, this season, this year)
- What surprised, inspired, or challenged me today?
- What worked today? What's working in my life?
- Is my curiosity stronger than my self-critic in this situation?
- What are the stories I'm telling myself that are not true?
- Where am I generous of spirit, not expecting anything in return?
- Where am I in competition or comparing myself with others?

Also, see the section on gratitude for tracking the four aspects of gratitude. In 2011, Angeles noted that Pema Chodron recommended that tracking be gentle, but precise. Five qualities that we need every day can also be tracked daily:

- Courage is needed for leadership and to manifest what we want to be in the world. It is acting in spite of fear and standing by what we believe in.
- Flexibility is resourcefulness and adaptability, while staying within one's own integrity.
- Integrity is being oneself, clear, and present.

- Trust is an inner quality, not related to thought—when we over-think, we are not trusting ourselves.
- Patience is at the center, the place of integration, where we work through all our issues with compassion and in nature's own time. It's typically easier to track impatience than patience.

Transformational Change. This level of change is a breakthrough—it fosters a major change in perspective, breaks old patterns, and represents new choices. A transformative change is visible and others will comment on the change in the transformed person.

Transitions. Angeles focused on the four (and sometimes 5) major transitions that most people experience throughout life: transitions in relationships, finances, health, or work/creativity arenas. In some of my notes, a fifth transition is identity/role changes. Many of us are in multiple transitions at any point in time. Life is a long series of transitions of varying lengths and intensities. Angeles noted that humans have a relentless drive toward wholeness, and that the human spirit seeks growth and integration. This requires us to consider who we are beyond our identities and roles and what we do. We are remembered for our personhood, not our accomplishments.

The Trickster. The trickster is an animal, person, or symbol that appears in our life to shake us up, stir us to an awakened state, or point out important lessons we need to learn.

Truth. What is the good, the beautiful, and the true in our nature? Angeles used the word true or truth to represent our authentic self, as in being true to ourselves. In 2005, Angeles quoted Sartre "Like all dreamers, I confuse disenchantment with truth."

What "T" words speak to you? What is your work at this time?

U is for Unbecoming

Angeles often talked about what it meant to be a mature adult, or to be in the second half of life where we come into our wisdom years. She would talk about having some immature behavior as being "less than becoming." For example, if you are hiding your true self or comparing yourself to others, that is "less than becoming." If you indulge in a pity party for months after a break-up, that is less than becoming behavior. Her whole philosophy was based on the importance of us all being mature and responsible adults. That did not mean being boring or no fun; she was the perfect model for how a sense of humor and a commitment to play and childlike wonder were compatible with being a responsible adult. But acting like a child in other ways than play and an attitude of awe and wonder is problematic.

Some of us actively resist aging through plastic surgery, cosmetics, and immature behaviors. We become over-identified with the physical signs of youth and physical appearance, and forfeit our wisdom, the real mark of maturity. Any issues that we resisted dealing with in our earlier life, will return to us to be dealt with now; what we do not integrate repeats itself until we finally address it. So being a mature adult means to accept the aging process with grace and flexibility and appreciate the good things it brings us.

Some of my most unbecoming behaviors have expressed in intimate relationships. For years, I endured an unfulfilling relationship with a person who was addicted to intensity. She lacked trust, constantly tested the relationship, and vacillated between drama and collapse, seeming to crave attention. Her neediness had initially drawn me into the relationship, as I was cursed with a thoroughly unbecoming tendency to be a rescuer in my youth. I suffered from the delusion that I could "fix" her and that my love would cast out all of her insecurities. When I finally came to my senses, instead of breaking off the relationship immediately, I engaged a wide array of "conduct unbecoming" of my age and life experience. I was afraid that she could not handle the truth, as she had engaged in self-harm in the past and threatened it often in the present. I also felt bound by the commitment I had made to see the relationship through times of sickness and health. Instead of having the courage to admit that I had made a mistake, and that this relationship was bad for both of us, I withdrew my love and affection slowly over time, appeased, endured in silence (not the noble kind of silence, but the passive-aggressive silent-treatment type) and went physically and emotionally AWOL from the relationship. When I finally decided I must leave the relationship, instead of talking to her directly, for several months I talked about the relationship behind her back to a couple of close friends. It took me a year to do the right thing in the right way, but I caused a lot of harm to both of us in the interim.

Now, looking back, I can see how weak-hearted I was, how conflict avoidant, and how many delusions I suffered: that I could change her, that her happiness depended on my behavior, that she could not handle me being truthful, that I was responsible for the failed relationship (because I could not get her to trust me). In retrospect, I can see all the flaws in my reasoning at the time. As I slowly mature and shed myself of some of these immature behaviors, I reflect on why I stayed in the relationship so long. Why didn't I have the courage to end it sooner? I realized that I invested so much effort into pleasing others and appearing a certain way as a leader and role model in my community. I could not face the idea of friends and community knowing that I had another failed relationship. So I put on a false mask and totally lost myself.

I'm a bit wiser now, but I still lapse into less than becoming behaviors on a regular basis. The difference is that I recognize them sooner and can course-correct, and I have developed more authentic ways of relating to other people that do not put me in situations where I lapse as much. I forgive myself when I do lapse and try to learn from the experience. Like so much of the work with Angeles, I have learned to strive for excellence, not perfection. If I shift my ratio of unbecoming behavior to mature adult behavior even a little, I'm making progress. Progress is not a breakthrough, though, so I'll keep on tracking and changing.

When was a time when your less than becoming behavior caused problems for you?

"U" Glossary

Uncertainty. This is a state of unknowing and indecisiveness. It is an uncomfortable state for those of us who like to feel in control and know where we are going next. Angeles urged us to sit with uncertainty and take no actions until we reach some place of clarity. When in uncertain territory, we can truly say, "I don't know" and be patient for the answers to appear. In other words, it is possible to have clarity about uncertainty. We can acknowledge that we are in this space and therefore cannot make a decision yet.

Unfamiliar. The word means "not of my family." We often stay in our comfort zone, our family, rather than choose the unfamiliar and unknowable where true creativity lies.

Unknowable. Many things in life are unknowable, belonging to the mystery. It requires much trust to know that we can handle whatever is ahead of us. To grow and create, we have to be willing to step into the unknowable. If we approach the new with wonder and awe, we can avoid a tendency to try to turn it into something knowable.

Unmentionables/Undiscuss-ables. These are the taboo topics in a relationship or a setting (such as a work site). If we cannot discuss these topics, the relationship moves into a polite, deadened state or a field of landmines to be carefully avoided, and resentment may begin to grow. Some people will pick fights just to see if the other person still cares.

Upset. This is a normal feeling, but not very specific. Often we need time to sort out why we are upset, especially for those of us who are slow processors. When upset, that is not the time to make decisions or take actions.

What "U" words speak to you? What is your work at this time?

V is for Vision

"Those who cannot vision will perish"

The visionary is the archetype of the east, where we let go of striving, resisting, and the false-self system. When we are willing to be our authentic selves, unlimited creativity is possible. Conflict avoidance is one large barrier to being authentic. Conflict avoiders are controllers, appeasers, or sometimes both at different times. The visionary is associated with the summer. The bright light of summer makes the shadow even darker and more defined—it shows where we are not in congruence with our true selves. Some questions to ask ourselves in the summer are:

- Am I willing to see things as they are rather than as I want them to be?
- Where are my pockets of authenticity and where do I avoid being authentic because of a fear of loss?
- What do I settle for, rather than address?
- Where do I tell the truth?

In one of the early weekend workshops I did with Angeles, she put us in dyads and had us do this visioning activity. She said that visioning had three parts or stages: making, catching, and weaving. Here is the exercise.

Vision Catching Activity:
Step one: This part involves writing in a journal: What do I want my life to look like 5 years from now? Consider relationship, family, community, nation, and world. Angeles noted that there is an "ask and you shall receive" type of saying in every wisdom tradition. This is vision making.

Step two. Pair with another person—that person closes their eyes and thinks about their life in five years and you merely observe them, and then share what you see as their future. This is vision catching. Now you close your eyes and think about your future life, and the other person shares what they see in you.

Step three. Consider what the other person said about your future and determine if it needs to be woven into your own plan. This is vision weaving.

All these stories are your own visions—what you initially create, what the other person sees in you and what you see in them, and what you re-imagine weaving together the visions. I must have it in myself to see it in another. What is strong in me will resonate with others and can be witnessed. What I dream I can create for myself.

This was one of those times when I saw the magic in Angeles' teaching. At first, when we started this activity, I thought it was ridiculous. What could I learn about someone's life dream by just looking at them? How could I possibly know what dreams a complete stranger might have? Yet when I looked at this stranger, I did manage to find something to say. It turned out that some of those things were part of the other person's vision, and other things I said were a surprise to the person, but resonated.

We all have some common links, like wanting to have a significant other relationship that is deep and loving, wanting harmony in our families, wanting an end to war and strife in the world and being a better steward to the earth. When she reported what she saw in me, much of what she said made sense to me. I might not have articulated them in my initial vision statement, but they were true of me. She said things about love of color and nature, and a desire for a lack of drama in my life. Afterwards, I wondered how Angeles had thought of this activity, and how often it worked out like this. What a gift Angeles had for asking the right questions or presenting information in a way that sparked self-discovery rather than being handed information.

Are you living the life you were sent here to live? If not, what type of re-visioning do you need at this time?

"V" Glossary

Validation. This is another of the arms of love. When we validate ourselves and other people, we confirm that we have heard and seen them and accept them as they are. We say, "you are important to me and I value you." The word valid refers to truth, so we are acknowledging that we see the "good and the true" in others and ourselves.

Victimhood. Playing the victim is a ploy for attention and puts the onus on others to give me what I need, or it involves asking others to tell me what my gifts are. If I am in sufficiency, I don't need attention and can relate to others as equals.

Vigilance. This means "holding a vigil unto oneself" or in other words, staying awake and present and being disciplined.

Violence. Angeles often said that all violence originates in the doubting, self-critical voices. Reducing violence in the outer world begins by keeping our self-critic in check and softening our judgments about ourselves and others.

Visible. Something that is visible can be seen, detected by our senses. Sometimes we hide our true selves or edit our thoughts so our true perceptions and core values are not visible, even to ourselves. Becoming visible is a leadership trait; standing up for oneself and being seen by others. The leader is fully present in the moment, and is visible. Sometimes we have gifts and talents that are hidden; these too, must be made visible to manifest.

Vision Quest. In the season of the visionary, Angeles arranged for groups to take vision quests, an immersion experience in solitude and silence in nature settings. Staying still in nature slows the body to nature's rhythm and allows the wisdom voice to emerge. Many people never or rarely have the luxury of 3 days and 2 nights totally alone and in silence. Angeles always asked us to pay attention to what our work was around three issues: self, relationship, and community/group. Questions to ask ourselves around these issues are:

- What is being strengthened, deepened, softened, and opened in my nature this year? What have I been resisting?
- What is the heart of my work in relationship at this time? What is the work I have avoided or resisted doing?
- How am I showing up in groups or communities at this time? How do I work in collaborations or in my family?

When we enter sacred land for vision quest, the five life energies of the land support us for healing, transformation, creative manifestation, integration, and initiation. A vision quest begins a few days before we go onto the land, and continues for a few days after we return. The vision quest keeps "working us" for days. It is important to pay attention to the seeds of learning during vision quest, note when others can see the changes in us (when they become witness-able), and integrate the experience so we don't forget.

Vulnerability. This concept is tied to authenticity. If we are not being ourselves in a relationship, we often engage in drama (exaggeration, looping, attention seeking) or collapse (becoming too emotional to cope). Being vulnerable is bringing forward your true self, saying what is so when it's so, without blame or judgment. We dare to be ourselves in the face of fear of rejection by loved ones.

What "V" words speak to you? What is your work at this time?

W is for Wisdom

The primary resource of the teacher archetype is wisdom, which hinges on the ability to see the world from a caring, but detached position. I had never linked wisdom with detachment prior to working with Angeles. She proposed that attachment to certain outcomes prevents us from hearing the wisdom voice--that voice that draws on our years of experience, intuition, and reflection that becomes integrated into a clear, declarative inner voice. If we have an attachment, a fixed perspective, we are no longer able to see the alternatives. The opposite of attachment is flexibility and curiosity, hallmarks of wisdom.

The wisdom way is calm, centered, even, reliable, and congruent. It does not explain, defend, rationalize, appease, seduce, or strategize. It aligns with compassion, fairness, and detachment. It does not indulge negative patterns in self, or in others, but instead, asks them with compassion "What action do you need to take to get back into balance?" The wise do not give advice, but help others to find their own solutions. This is a totally different image than the idea of the wise person I had when I was younger. I imagined someone who could freely give advice and set me on the right path. Angeles had a knack for defying this stereotype with humor. Whenever someone asked her an either/or question; "Should I do X or Y?" She would simply say, "Yes."

The wisdom voice is never mean-spirited, petty, critical, or over-analytical. It is simple and declarative. It does not take a lot of words to state the truth. Think of aphorisms: those pithy phrases that capture an important point in a phrase or a sentence. Some examples of aphorisms are:

> Wise men talk because they have something to say; fools because they have to say something (Plato).

> Forgiveness is the fragrance that the violet sheds on the heel that has crushed it (Mark Twain).

> Some cause happiness wherever they go; others whenever they go (Oscar Wilde)

If we are embellishing and rationalizing, we are building a case and speaking from the ego, not the heart. The heart's voice is the wisdom voice. When I despair over ever becoming wise myself, I remember Angeles' words "Where we are is the way through." I have to trust that where I am right now, is where I should be, but not where I will always be. I have to be patient, keep practicing curiosity and track where I get attached, and things will shift.

Questions to foster the development of wisdom include:

- What ignites my desire to learn?
- What triggers giving up? Most things don't work optimally the first time—why do I give up so quickly?
- How do I take direction from others? Do I rebel? Defiance is not a place of learning.
- How do I give direction to others? What is my tone? (pay attention to the content as well as the tone). Am I giving advice?
- Where am I over-identified in a role or identity?
- Where do I lack discipline?

Components of wisdom include clarity, objectivity (nonattachment to outcome), fair self-talk, curiosity, and discernment. A wise person is able to ask for help from others, or the ancestors. The wisdom way is a place of learning, reflection, and contemplation. It is a middle path between drama and collapse, and between control and appeasement. Wisdom is connected to my authentic nature. Equanimity is an example of a middle path between good and bad—it accepts things as they are. The wisdom way involves some containment of extremes to be able to stay on the middle path.

Maria Popova, author of a website called Brainpickings, described the difference between information, knowledge, and wisdom. She said we are "awash" in a sea of information, which contains isolated bits and pieces of facts and opinions. As we assemble the facts, we can gain knowledge as we see how certain bits of information fit together. We start to identify patterns. But wisdom is beyond just knowledge, and has a moral aspect to it. Wisdom is not only knowledge, but also principles about how that knowledge should be used in the world for the greatest good. That is where Angeles' principle of "be open to outcome, not attached," is critical. We need that detachment to see the potential consequences of applying knowledge in different situations, and to recognize that knowledge is not neutral. We can use our power for the most ethical application of knowledge that serves the great good. We cannot be wise without developing character qualities of compassion, honesty, and love.

So how do we move from knowledge to wisdom? Angeles recommended sitting meditation, silence in nature, and slowing down our rhythm to "slow to medium" so that we can reflect and integrate knowledge into a deeper wisdom that accesses all three locations of body wisdom: the mind, the heart, and the gut/intuition. We have to track our experiences so that we have seeds of learning to plant. As those seeds grow and we integrate them into our daily lives along with our character, we can harvest wisdom.

How am I fostering my own development of wisdom at this time? Where am I attached to outcome so that I foreclose my own wisdom?

"W" Glossary

WAIT. This stands for "Why Am I Talking?" It is a practice to make us stop and think about whether I am speaking truth, whether the time and place are right, and whether I should be listening rather than talking.

Walking Meditation. This type of meditation is good for problem-solving. You put the question before you, then start to walk, focusing on the breath or taking slow deliberate steps to get into a rhythm or zone that breaks the monkey mind pattern of constant internal chatter. Listen to the birds, the break of waves, the wind in the trees, and soon the solution to the problem will come to you. Walking meditation is a tool of the visionary, and physically opens the body to the flow of ideas. Angeles said, "If you want an answer, go for a walk."

Witnessing. This is the process of seeing and validating another person in their vulnerability or when they make a vow to change some old pattern or break out of their comfort zone. Witnessing is a powerful process, beyond just observing something. When we witness another's pain, we grow in compassion; when we witness their commitments to change, we are part of their sacred intention and can help hold them accountable. Angeles said "What we witness, we are changed by. When we are witnessed, we cannot go back to old ways."

Work. We are best placed in work that aligns with our values and has heart and meaning for us. As Gibran said, "Work is love made visible." And Rumi said, "Let the beauty of what you love be what you do." Work is one of the life transitions that works us. We get to apply all the teachings that Angeles gave us in our work or creative endeavors. It is a great practice ground for warrior, healer, teacher, and visionary work.

Woundology. Angeles' pointed out that people in indigenous cultures rarely had mental illnesses and proposed that it was because they had a very different interpretation of traumatic events in their lives. They perceive these events as initiations along life's path, and experiences that shaped them, but do not control them. They recognize that responses we have to trauma when we are young come out of the more limited resources we had then. If we behave the same way as adults, we are indulging old patterns. In the western world, we see the early traumas as deep, unheal-able wounds and often do not recognize that we have choices to behave differently now. We can forgive, tool up, and behave like adults. To stay in the place of suffering and insufficiency is to follow the path of woundology.

Another thing to consider is that if one breaks a bone, the scar tissue that results from healing is stronger than the original bone. If we can transfer this idea to our mental health, we can think of ourselves as growing stronger when we heal from trauma.

In a workshop on mentoring (2010), Angeles presented a model for healing psychological wounds. The process is called APRI, which comes from Jungian analysts. Apri, in Italian, means "for you." This process stands for:

> A = addressing the issue,
> P = processing the issue (with a professional, not your friends),
> R = resolving the issue (taking actions toward healing and change; may be negatively impacted by attachments),
> I = integrating the issue so that it does not keep affecting your life.

Friends cannot help with the processing phase of such issues, because friends give agreement, not growth. Once we have resolved and integrated the issue, we will have a witness-able change in our behavior.

What "W" words speak to you? What is your work at this time?

X is for Xtra Love

X is a hard letter—not many words start with X and I cannot remember any that come from Angeles' teaching. On the other hand, there is one phrase that fits here. Sometimes a person got a bit of a grilling from Angeles, done in the most gentle, yet firm manner, of course. Louis Rosenbaum, one of the extraordinary members of the *Four Fold Way*™ community and an anchor of every year-long program I was in, spoke of it as "extra love." He recognized that Angeles was helping the person dig deeper into painful or unknown territory. If you really have high regard and love for another person, you are willing to help them find out their own truths, get vulnerable, and identify unhealthy patterns or old wounds. The role of a true mentor is to help others to identify their own patterns, and sometimes that is a bit painful.

In one session, I got that extra loving. Angeles had been telling some story of the man who co-wrote the *Chicken Soup for the Soul* series of books—books that offer healing stories from every day people. The first book manuscript that they submitted was rejected by dozens of publishers, but the authors persisted until they found the right match. Soon after this story, Angeles posed a question about issues that were affecting us now, and where we had given up prematurely. I made a flippant remark about writing a book based on my experience in relationships called "Chicken Soup for the Chicken-Hearted." Angeles looked at me with such sad eyes—I thought I even saw a little tear form, and she gently probed me about my use of humor to deflect attention from issues that deeply troubled me. She gave me much to think about—was I also using humor as a way to seek approval and attention from others in the group? Was I focused on being clever rather than being vulnerable? The two or three minutes that Angeles focused on me had a profound effect for weeks to come, and produced some insights about my fears of sharing more deeply in group settings.

Have you had an experience that opened you up to more vulnerability? What teachers in your life cared enough to help you see yourself more clearly?

X Glossary

What "X" words speak to you? What is your work at this time?

Y is for Yielding

"Be like bamboo. Firm but yielding."

This concept is related to flexibility. A bamboo reed is strong, almost unbreakable, because it can yield in the wind. It bends to adapt to pressure. Strength as a personhood quality is not rigid or absolute, but has a fluid and yielding kind of power. Yielding does not mean to give up one's power in this context, but rather to increase one's power.

Yielding also means to give up resistance and turn one's self over to the mystery. To do this, we have to trust in ourselves, trust in others, and trust in the circumstances. Yielding means to give up attempts to control.

In the world of finance, a yield is also defined as a return on investments made. Working with Angeles' tools will have tremendous yields. This is the definition that I want to focus on here. As I mentioned in the introduction, I did not fully commit to this work in the first two years after being exposed to it. I knew that it would require a major transformation, and I was in the stressful transition of settling into a new job, new apartment, new geographical region, and was making new friends and grieving the loss of my old life. I could not commit to a rigorous practice at that time because I was overwhelmed with adjusting to all these changes. But I had experienced enough of the program that the ideas did guide me through that challenging time, and as soon as I felt settled in my new life, I committed to my first "year-long" program with Angeles. From that point on, I was mostly committed, with brief periods of doubts and relapses. I started incorporating the teaching into my daily life. Once into the work, I realized that life was the practice of Angeles' teaching. I did not have to set aside time each week to "practice," because everything I did all day long was a practice. I tried to bring the teachings into my relationships with family and friends, into my teaching at a university, into the way I interacted with co-workers, and the way I spent my leisure time. The yields have been incredibly rich and rewarding. If Angeles' teachings were an investment on Wall Street, they would represent the ones that produce nothing but positive gains. There is absolutely nothing to lose. And if you engage and buy enough stock, you will have tremendous wealth that keeps growing as long as you live.

What yields have you experienced from working with Angeles' tools and teaching?

"Y" Glossary

Yeah-Buts. Angeles told of the nay-sayers in our lives that would respond to any suggestion we made with a "Yeah, but that won't work" kind of answer. She called them the "Yeah-but family." One activity that Angeles had us do to address this type of response was in groups of three: One tells about a challenging situation where they feel stuck. The other two listen to the situation, and then one acts as the positive voice: the "I can" deal with this. The other is the "yeah-but" negative voice. Those two dialogue in front of the one with the situation. This brings the pros and cons discussion that we often have in our heads out into the open so we can witness it with a bit more detachment. Or you can think of it as a dialogue between the wisdom voice and the self-critic.

Year-End Reflections. Angeles pointed out the value of assessing one's year in the transition between fall and winter. Some questions to ask are:

- What have I released this year?
- What parts of my false self have I let go of this year?
- What has not come to fruition? What do I need to let go of?
- What has manifested this year?
- What has deepened or come together?
- Where have I been inspired/challenged/surprised?
- What have I learned about love this year?
- What breakthroughs have I had this year?
- What has made me happy this year?

We need to reflect and integrate this information in order to end the year well, and be in good position to start a new year. Winter is a good time for solitary reflection (hibernation) and integrating the experiences of the past year. These questions help one identify what work we have done in the past year, and what work still needs to be done in the coming year.

Yes. Sometimes it is good to just say yes to life and love and beauty! On the other hand, Angeles noted that in western cultures, we say yes to mean "I like you" and "I agree with you." In other parts of the world, it only means "I acknowledge your viewpoint." It does not mean a personal approval. No is an acknowledgement of a limit and boundary. Angeles often said "No is a complete sentence." You can ask yourself, "With whom, and where, do I have difficulty saying no?" This may indicate approval needs or competition. When we say yes when we don't really mean it, we are withholding the truth or appeasing. It's an act of arrogance because it assumes that the other person cannot handle the truth.

What "Y" words speak to you? What is your work at this time?

Z is for Zen

I never actually heard Angeles use this term, but it seems a fitting way to end the glossary of teaching words, because it is an apt description of Angeles' personhood and the experience of sitting in a circle at her feet. According to the dictionary, zen is a form of Buddhism that arose in China, but proliferated in 6th century Japan as a spiritual tradition that uses meditation to achieve a form of enlightenment. Angeles' program used many forms of meditation and a host of other practices to help us become enlightened, balanced, well-developed characters. But I would like to explore Angeles' being as a trait; a state of mind/body rather than a philosophy.

In this context, zen is a state of being that is enlightenment embodied: an integration of mind, body, and spirit. It is an alignment of heart, mind, and gut. The person who is a zen master exudes a sense of peace, calm, and harmony. Zen seems to be akin to the concept of equanimity, or staying in the calm center rather than lapsing into disturbance or excess.

I sat in group one evening fuming internally. One participant was talking, sharing a story that was an ongoing issue for her. I had heard it many times, and I had heard Angeles give this woman tips about shape-shifting, about letting go, about giving up control, and about how damaging holding on to old stories could be. Angeles had just finished asking the woman to stay "present-forward" and state the seeds of her learning about this event. The woman seemed to have internalized none of this, and continued in a self-deprecating, insufficient manner to blame herself and another for this issue. She was stuck, looping in the story.

I watched Angeles closely, waiting for her to come down hard on this woman and accuse her of not listening, or not applying the years of teaching she had in Angeles' circle. At the very least, I expected to see some eye-rolling or other sign of annoyance or frustration that the other woman was still "not getting it." But all I saw was "mountain countenance." Angeles showed no sign of any emotion, and instead, tried again to help this woman get out of story and gain some perspective or discover an action to change the situation. Her response was beyond patience. In all the years I worked with Angeles, I never saw her lose her temper, show irritation, or ignore an annoying person or comment. She continued to do what she always did. She taught by healing stories and asking questions. She did not give up on people. Was Angeles the ultimate enlightened being? I don't know the answer to this, but she certainly came as close to it as any person I've ever met.

Who have been your teachers of enlightenment? Who has modeled this "zen-like" quality for you?

Z Glossary

Zest. Angeles often talked about having zest for life, in terms of the fires of vision and creativity, of maintaining awe and wonder for the world, and approaching new tasks with a childlike enthusiasm.

What "Z" words speak to you? What is your work at this time?

Afterword

In the process of reflecting on my years of work with Angeles, I have tried to figure out what made her such an influential teacher and mentor to so many people around the world. What was it about her that put her in a realm far above good teacher, or effective mentor? Some of it came from her unique background that made her a cross-cultural bridger.

She was very private about her personal life, but over the years, she shared a few facts about her path in life. She was born in Spain into a community of Basque sheepherders. Her parents moved to Idaho when she was young, but she lived part-time in Spain and part-time in Idaho most of her youth—her family was in the U.S with a three year visa so they had to return to Spain at least every three years. This provided much opportunity to observe the differences and similarities in the two diverse cultures in which she was raised. She was sent out on a year-long vision quest in the Pyrenee Mountains when she was 16. She studied cultural anthropology at UC Berkeley and had two very influential mentors; first Margaret Mead and then later, Joseph Campbell. She was called to teaching in her early 30s, and from then on, taught the *Four Fold Way*™ among many other things. She was an itinerant teacher, working at many different colleges in the bay area. She never thought of herself as a writer, yet she completed several highly influential books in her lifetime. She dictated all of her books to preserve her gift as a storyteller. Some of these books have been translated into multiple languages for international audiences.

Those are facts about her life, but what about the quality she called "personhood"? It was her being, as much as her doing, that made her a unique teacher and role model. I've tried to catalog the qualities of her personhood that made her such a potent teacher and mentor. Some of those are:

- She was the most authentic person I ever met. She walked her talk and lived her life according to her teachings, a true living and breathing role model.

- She was in service to others; her ego never appeared in her teaching, yet she modeled self-care and sufficiency.

- She used her power wisely and for the good of others, not for her own gain. She wanted her teaching to be about the lessons, not her as the teacher.

- She had a palpable presence, but one that was accessible and modeled right use of power.

- She was available to all who sought her help and never showed favoritism.

- She saw the good in every one.

- She had a phenomenal memory, so that she remembered everyone's name and their stories.

- She rarely gave advice, but instead, helped each person access their own inner wisdom voice and freely gave away tools for a better life.

- She never took credit for her wisdom and teachings, but instead, always gave credit and gratitude to her teachers: parents and family, community, important strangers, indigenous wisdom texts and teachers, and the ancestors. She was a conduit for ancient wisdom. She put her unique spin on these teachings, but did not assume to "own" them. She did not "hold back" her gifts and talents but freely expressed them to the benefit of all. I never heard her refer to the *Four Fold Way*™ as "my" program.

- She had a gentle sense of humor and a twinkle in her eye. Her humor, like her style of teaching, was kind.

In other words, she embodied all those concepts that she taught: patience, compassion, flexibility, curiosity, equanimity, courage, kindness, and so many more. Although many of us called her "teacher," she was a truly balanced warrior, visionary, healing teacher.

Angeles Arrien (December 25, 1940-April 24, 2014) was original medicine, not anywhere else duplicated. She touched the lives of so many people through her teaching and her books, and her example. May we all aspire to follow her on the "mystical path with practical feet."

Resources

Books by Angeles Arrien:

Angeles Arrien (1993). *The Four Fold Way: Walking the paths of the Warrior, Teacher, Healer and Visionary*. San Francisco: HarperSanFrancisco.

Angeles Arrien (1997). *The tarot handbook: Practical applications of ancient visual symbols.* New York, NY: Jeremy Tarcher/Putnam.

Angeles Arrien (1998). *Signs of life: The five universal shapes and how to use them.* NY, NY: Jeremy Tarcher/Putnam.

Angeles Arrien (2000). *The nine muses: A mythological path to creativity.* New York, NY: Jeremy Tarcher/Putnam.

Angeles Arrien (2001). *Working together: Diversity as opportunity.* San Francisco: Berrett-Koehler Publishers.

Angeles Arrien (2005). *The second half of life: Opening the eight gates of wisdom.* Boulder, CO: Sounds True.

Angeles Arrien (2011). *Living in gratitude.* Boulder, CO: Sounds True.

Books that Angeles often recommended:

Ted Andrews (2004). *Animal speak: the spiritual and magical powers of creatures great and small.* St Paul, MN: Llewellyn Press.

David Richo (1991). *How to be an adult.* Mahway, NJ: Paulist Press.

David Richo (2009). *How to be an adult in relationships.* Self-published.

Peter Felton, H-Dirksen Bauman, Aaron Kheriaty, and Edward Taylor (2013). *Transformative conversations: A guide to mentoring communities among colleagues in higher education.* San Francisco: Wiley. (Angeles contributed to the forward and afterword, and served as a mentor to the authors).

Made in the USA
Middletown, DE
10 April 2023

28593027R00102